MODERN

MODERN FALCONRY

*Your Illustrated Guide to
the Art and Sport of Hunting
with North American Hawks*

Jack Samson

Illustrations by Victoria Blanchard

Stackpole Books

Copyright © 1984 by Stackpole Books

Published by
STACKPOLE BOOKS
Cameron and Kelker Streets
P.O. Box 1831
Harrisburg, PA 17105

Printed in the U.S.A.

Library of Congress Cataloging in Publication Data

Samson, Jack.
   Modern falconry.

   Bibliography: p.
   Includes index.
   1. Falconry—United States.   I. Title.
SK321.S27   1984   799.2′32   84-2610
ISBN 0-8117-2158-2

Contents

Foreword

IN THE MID-1930s, Jack Samson had charge of the live hawks, falcons, and owls at New York's Bear Mountain State Park outdoor wildlife interpretive exhibitions operated by the American Museum of Natural History. Peregrine falcons still nested then — long before DDT spread its curse over the land — on nearby Storm King Mountain and on the Palisades of the Hudson River within sight of New York City.

Jack was not content to maintain his charges in cages. Happiness for him was to walk about with everything from red-shouldered hawks to great horned owls perched on his wrist. With great patience and skill in conditioning the birds, he devised a system of displaying them in the open by preparing soft leather jesses for their legs, and tethering them to padded perches or blocks, where they soon learned to be comfortable and ceased trying to escape. Thus, he was adapting an age-old method used by falconers to keep their trained birds in good shape. The birds were apt to break their feathers and otherwise injure themselves if kept behind wire. Several zoos used Jack's method in later years, not alone for the welfare of the birds, but also because the public enjoyed seeing them without intervening wires or bars.

Leading falconers from the American Museum of Natural History visited the Bear Mountain bird exhibition and passed on their information to the young man in charge who soon became an authority in his own right, spending much of his time on the scientific study of raptorial species — their behavior in and out of captivity, their food requirements, nesting and flight habits, and other details essential to a rounded and thorough knowledge of the birds that had captivated him. His interest in falcons and falconry has persisted through the years, fostering a type of intimate relationship between bird and man that originated some two thousand years before Christ.

> William H. Carr
> *Curator, Arizona-Sonora*
> *Desert Museum, Tucson, Arizona*

Introduction

THIS BOOK MAKES no pretense at being a definitive work of falconry. There are a number of those — several American, but mostly European.

What this book does try to do is give the beginner — the novice at falconry in North America — an idea of what the sport is and how to go about it. *Modern Falconry* does attempt to discuss the various types of North American hawks that might make good hunters, and how to train them. Recognizing that the average beginning falconer on this continent will not be able to obtain either a peregrine falcon or a gyrfalcon very easily, I have attempted to keep the book within the reach of the average person, and for that reason discuss the hawks he or she is likely to get.

This book is being updated and published at this time because of the very real need of a timely, comprehensive, and inexpensive manual on North American falconry.

There are two books in the United States on the subject that are really excellent, but they are hard to get and expensive. Most beginning falconers have never heard of them and have a rather poor chance of locating them. They are: *North American Falconry and Hunting Hawks*, by Frank Beebe and Harold Webster. It was printed by World Press,

Inc., Denver, Colorado in 1964. Because I got to know Hal Webster and admire him, I was able to get a copy. It sold then for about $25. Twelve years later, in 1976, Frank Beebe, a fine ornithologist, writer, and artist, came out with his own book, *Hawks, Falcons and Falconry*, Hancock House, Publishers, Ltd., Saanichton, B.C., Canada; Seattle, Washington; and New York. This book also sold for about $25 at the time of publication. Both these books should be considered classics in Northern American falconry literature.

If you are interested in learning about hawks, eagles, and falcons in general, Leslie Brown and Dean Amadon's monumental *Eagles, Hawks & Falcons of the World*, McGraw-Hill, New York, 1968, cannot be surpassed for information.

There are two other American books published on hawks and falconry that I would recommend as fine reading. One is *Falcon's Return*, a book on restoring an endangered species, by John Kaufmann and that marvelous falconer and ornithologist, Heinz Meng. I had the opportunity of knowing Heinz Meng when I lived in New York, as editor of *Field & Stream*, and found him a charming man as well as a fine falconer. The other book is a modest publication titled *The World of the Red-Tailed Hawk*, by G. Ronald Austing, J.B. Lippincott Co., Philadelphia and New York, 1964. A Park Service ranger, Ron Austing turned a lifelong interest in hawks into a delightful book, filled with information and photos of hawks.

The rest of the fine books on falconry have been written and printed in Europe, India, and the Near East. They are listed in the bibliography in the back of this book.

If I had to recommend any European book on falconry, I think I would pick M.H. Woodford's *A Manual of Falconry*, Adam & Charles Black, London, 1966. It is concise and readable and sells at a reasonable price. It is relatively free of obscure English terminology.

The reason *Modern Falconry* was written dates from an incident in 1975. While the editor of *Field & Stream*, I decided to publish two articles on falconry, simultaneously — one, "Hunting with Goshawks, by a very knowledgeable falconer, Chuck Keene, of Cornwall, New York, and another, "Hunting with Falcons," by past-president of the California Hawking Club, Ray Linder.

Both stories brought a tremendous amount of reader mail. They also brought down upon both falconers and me a considerable amount of wrath from some falconers in the North American Falconry Association. It seems they did not want falconry revealed to the general public in that way, and they thought it a crime for any publication to encourage beginners and young people to get involved with the sport. Falconry, in

Europe, had long been associated with the privileged class, and I suspect it was still thought of that way in America by certain individuals.

Some of the reader mail took exception to falconry under the misguided assumption that it is a "cruel" sport. I dismissed these letters from "protectionists," having been exposed to them for years as editor of a magazine concerned with hunting and fishing. After all, a hawk or falcon kills by instinct and does so in nature to survive. If that is cruel, all nature is cruel.

But the overwhelming bulk of mail came from American youngsters. In a six month's period following publication of those two articles in *Field & Stream*, we received in excess of 30,000 letters asking for more information on falconry! That told me something.

It apparently told other people, too. Since then, the federal government and the various states have made giant strides in recognizing falconry as a legitimate sport. Today, if you are serious about becoming a falconer, you can read about the sport, take an examination to become an apprentice falconer, get your own hawk, and practice the art. The situation today is light years away from what it was in 1975 — when falconry was literally illegal in most states and was the domain of a few stuffy and elitest falconry groups.

One man who did not consider it wrong to teach youngsters about the sport was Heinz Meng — one of the several men in America credited with captive breeding of the endangered peregrine falcon and one who believes falconry has a great future in the hands of young people in the United States. He was happy to help with this book and has done much to bring the sport to young people. Chuck Keene has also been involved in teaching young people and new falconers about the sport. Tom Knight in Washington State is another, and Pete McLain of the New Jersey Department of Game & Fish has long supported public participation in the sport by the general public. And each year others join the ranks.

My awareness of the vital interest of young people in this ancient sport began early — as a teenager. I had an intense interest in the birds of prey, and I developed it by working with hawks, eagles, and owls at Trailside Museum in New York prior to World War II. Following the war, I attended the University of New Mexico in Albuquerque and had a chance to experiment with falconry again. I raised and flew sparrow hawks, goshawks, and prairie falcons in New Mexico.

With the outbreak of the Korean War, I began a five-year stint as a foreign correspondent in the Far East. While there, I became acquainted with falconers in Japan, India, and Southeast Asia. Beginning in 1955, I returned to New Mexico for 10 years as writer for the Associated Press, and again I had a chance to work my falcons.

During the late 1960s and 1970s—while I was editing *Field & Stream*, my sons grew up in the small town of Cape May, New Jersey. My youngest son, James, developed the same fascination for hawks that I did as a boy. I was able, by obtaining a permit to trap hawks in New Jersey, to get back into falconry again. Cape May was a lovely spot to observe hawks. It was on the main migration route of a great many hawks—including the few peregrine falcons that survived the DDT plague. My son became a good falconer in those years and still follows the sport. It was seeing his enthusiasm about falconry—and that of his school friends—that encouraged me to write this book.

The author gentles a captive-bred peregrine falcon. This species was hit hard by pesticides.

I am back in my beloved New Mexico today — as Editor-at-Large of *Field & Stream*. Falconry is alive and well in this state, as in many others today. The hawks are back in great numbers, protected against shooting and the ravages of pesticides. The states and the federal government not only allow the sport today but also actively encourage it. Falconry has come of age in America. I only hope this modest manual helps the beginner discover the joys of a sport that began thousands of years before the birth of Christ.

JACK SAMSON

Tom Smylie, one of the best falconers in North America, holds Charlotte, his female captive-reared Peale's peregrine. — Photo by Cherie Rife Smylie.

Acknowledgments

I AM INDEBTED to falconers Hal Webster and Heinz Meng for their patience and generosity in allowing me time to talk and an opportunity to photograph.

In addition I am also grateful for photographic help from such interested falconers as Tom Knight of the State of Washington Department of Fish and Game; Chuck Keene of Cornwall-on-Hudson, New York; Hal Webster; Dr. Meng; Margaret Nichols of *Field & Stream*; Teddy Schubert, biologist of the New Jersey Department of Environmental Protection for her vast knowledge of raptors; Director Russell A. Cookingham of the New Jersey Department of Environmental Protection for a state permit to trap hawks; Rex C. Tice of the Bureau of Sport Fisheries and Wildlife for a federal permit to trap raptors; Nat Reed, former assistant secretary of the Interior, for his efforts to publish new federal falconry regulations; to *Field & Stream* for permission to reprint photographs from an article entitled "Hunting with Hawks," January 1975; and to Tom Smylie and Jim Rous, U.S. Fish and Wildlife Service, for their help with the latest federal falconry regulations.

1

A Brief History
of Falconry

FALCONRY — HUNTING WITH hawks — is one of the few surviving hunting sports that dates to the earliest days of recorded human history. It was practiced in Asia — specifically in China — as long ago as 2,000 years before Christ. In Japan, it seems to have been known as early as 600 years B.C. In the Middle East — particularly in Arabia, Persia, and Syria — bas-reliefs dating from as long ago as 1,700 years B.C. picture falconers carrying hawks on their wrists.

I refer to falconry as a sport because even after the invention of the firearm — a far cheaper and more efficient method of securing waterfowl, upland game birds, and small game — falconry has been practiced much the same as in the days of the ancient Egyptians or the time after the Crusades, when Europeans introduced it to their native lands. Even more than horse racing, falconry could be called the true sport of kings. It was for ages the principal sport of the rich — probably because they were the only ones who could afford the birds and the upkeep of falconers, and who owned the vast lands and had the leisure time needed for the sport.

The oldest records of falconry in Europe appear to be those of Pliny and Aristotle. Their writings on the subject are somewhat vague but do show that the sport was popular in ancient Greece between 384 B.C. and 40 A.D. About 860 A.D., the sport was brought from the continent to England, where it flowered. The English took to falconry like Labrador retrievers to water, and no sport — not even fox hunting from horses — has ever gained the popularity that falconry did in the British Isles, especially during the seventeenth century. Strict laws governed the sport, with special attention given to it during the reigns of William the Conqueror, Edward III, Henry VIII, and Elizabeth I.

At one point, the sport was so regimented that birds of prey were allocated according to the degree of rank of their owners: to an emperor, the eagle; to kings and queens, the great northern gyrfalcons; to earls, the peregrine falcons; to a yeoman, a goshawk; to a lady, a merlin (our pigeon hawk); to a priest, a sparrow hawk (our sharp-shinned hawk of today) and, according to the *Encyclopaedia Britannica*, "to a knave or a servant, the useless kestrel." (The kestrel is our tiny American sparrow hawk.)

Falconry was much mentioned in the writings of William Shakespeare. Even today it is held in high esteem in England, although not practiced on the level it once was.

The history of falconry in America is altogether different. First of all, it never gained much popularity in the early Colonial days, probably because the nation was never ruled by a landed aristocracy. Most of the people who emigrated to America did so to get away from oppression by the very aristocrats who found falconry so appealing. It is possible the sport was associated with the "idle rich" of Europe and therefore had no place here. There were some devotees of the sport — a few wealthy Americans who had observed it abroad. But for most, it was far more simple to hunt with a fowling piece than with a falcon.

We are a people who saw the gun win the continent — from the struggles of the Pilgrims to the battles of the West. Largely an agricultural people, we developed the farmers' and ranchers' traditional antipathy toward predators. Wild creatures were divided into two categories: game to be hunted for food (and sport), and inedible wildlife that preyed upon game. Any wild creature thought to prey on livestock and poultry fell into the predator class. Predators were, and still are, widely feared, hated, and sought after for bounties. These creatures include mountain lions, wolves, coyotes, bobcats, hawks, eagles, owls, and even rodents.

I remember belonging to the old Square Circle Conservation Club sponsored by *Field & Stream* in the late 1930s. One of the articles we all swore to uphold was to fire a number of shells (I forget how many) per week or month at a hawk. Since all hawks were considered "chicken hawks" in those days, it amazes me that the birds of prey managed to survive. I can only attribute it to our terrible marksmanship.

For many years, when I was young and ignorant, I shot at the buteo hawks, the big, slow-flying, wide-winged hawks such as the Harris's hawk, the red-tailed hawk, the red-shouldered hawk, the zone-tailed hawk, Swainson's hawk, the broad-winged hawk, Sennet's white-tailed hawk, the rough-legged hawk, and the harrier or marsh hawk—plus all the kites, such as the Everglades kite, the Mississippi kite, the white-tailed kite, the swallow-tailed kite, and the eagles. I even shot at the unfortunate osprey, which I was convinced was catching all my trout and bass.

This Eskimo stone carving of a falcon is probably meant to represent a gyrfalcon.

The man who set me straight about which hawks did what to which birds was the legendary Warden Ted Townsend of Westchester County, New York. When he died during World War II, *The New Yorker* magazine did a two-part profile about him. Huge and rotund, he drove about White Plains and environs in an open touring car, carrying a lever-action rifle in a saddle scabbard and several shotguns on the seat beside him.

It was not until the 1950s and 1960s — when the ravages of DDT finally were brought home to all of us in an environmental awakening spurred by some great writing, such as Rachel Carson's *Silent Spring* — that we began to realize that shooting birds of prey was like removing sand from the desert a grain at a time compared to the wholesale slaughter by chemicals. The DDT worked its way from dead insects through the songbirds and shorebirds into the raptors — particularly the fish-eating osprey and the peregrine falcon — until the body chemistry was so badly affected that it interfered with the mating urges and the thickness of the eggshells. The shells would break when the nesting parent sat on the eggs. When an egg breaks, the parent bird either eats the broken egg or shoves it off the nest and lays more — only to have them break. The future of the raptors looked bleak indeed at the beginning of the 1960s, until conservationists and government experts won their battle to ban the deadly chemical pesticide. There have been setbacks, but by and large DDT has been banned within the limits of the continental United States. However, the hawks are still not free of the threat. Surplus DDT was sold to foreign countries, where the migrating songbird population absorbed it during winter months, as did the raptors that followed the normal food supply of waterfowl and smaller birds into Mexico and Central and South America.

Only just before World War II did falconers in the United States become known for their experiments with American hawks. When I first became acquainted with falconry and ran the raptor division of the American Museum of Natural History's Trailside Museum at Bear Mountain, New York, in the late 1930s and early 1940s, names associated with the sport included Frank and John Craighead, Heinz Meng, Hal Webster, Morley Nelson, and Frank Beebe. Some of them are still very much in the falconry picture — particularly Meng. Surprisingly, falconry during this period and into the 1970s gained an ardent following of young people, drawn by the nostalgic value as well as the pure hunting aspects of the sport. Falconry clubs sprang up across the United States, and many young people corresponded with European and Middle Eastern falconers. There is now a core of devoted young falconers, a large number in California.

The federal government — feeling the pressure from bird-watcher groups and uninformed and hysterical organizations devoted to prevent-

A female sparrow hawk is this beginner's first experience in the art and sport of falconry.

ing "cruelty to animals"—began to concern itself with setting down regulations for the sport. However, the regulations left much of the jurisdiction up to states, and many not only took a realistic attitude toward the hunting sport but encouraged it. Others did not.

There is every reason to believe that falconry, if practiced properly and with supervision, can be one of the finest sports available to the veteran and the youngster alike who love the outdoors and especially the great birds of prey.

2

Some Preliminaries

IT CAN BE a tough world today for a youngster who loves the birds of prey and is interested in the sport of falconry. When I was a kid, there were no laws governing the possession or capture of hawks, eagles, or owls. All we had to do was find them. Now there are all sorts of rules and regulations — federal, state, and local. Moreover, the proper practice of the sport itself has built-in demands and limitations to try the patience of those who lack determination.

The aim of this book is to help newcomers who are loaded with such determination to channel it toward the rewards of a deeply satisfying and thrilling sport.

First, anyone who wants to become a falconer must have access to plenty of room to train and exercise a bird. It is cruel to restrict a falcon or any other hunting hawk to a small, enclosed space, such as a city apartment. Falconry is not keeping a hawk just to carry about on a wrist. This is as idiotic as buying a high-spirited German short-haired pointer and keeping it in a one-room city apartment all its life. Yorkshire terriers and toy poodles make fine city dogs — if you must have a dog in the city. If you want a bird to carry around in a city, buy a parakeet.

If just owning a hawk is your aim, you should quit here. This is written for the serious falconer living in a rural area having access to plenty of open space. Moreover, falconry is time-consuming. The care and training of a hunting hawk takes several hours a day, especially in the early stages of training. Anyone who goes into the sport without adequate space and time is making a mistake.

One of the first things you must do is learn the law. Know the federal regulations (see Chapter 16) and check your individual state's codes. *Whatever you do must comply with these regulations.*

It is also a good idea to make friends with the state and federal game-management officials in your area. Many have expert knowledge of hawks and are eager to help beginners — to advise them on the nature of the laws and, since they spend much time in the field and know the whereabouts of hawks, to teach you about their habits and habitats. Moreover, such contacts often offer an opportunity to gain firsthand information because many injured hawks are turned over to game officials who may be happy to have some help in caring for them.

And now, about this book. I know only too well your eagerness to rush out and start hunting with your bird. Unfortunately, it can't happen that way. Some vital preliminaries must be attended to, such as learning falconry terms and becoming familiar with the equipment. If you either capture or purchase a hawk, it is necessary to have falconry equipment ready at home before the bird is brought back. You might prefer to skim through the language and equipment sections first and refer back to them later. But at least a once-over lightly may help spare you constant checking for definitions when you get into the more exciting chapters about trapping and hunting the birds.

You should also devote some time to the section that deals with the hunting hawks and their field habits. All this preliminary information is necessary if you are to do right by yourself and your bird when you get into trapping, training, and hunting.

Further on are sections on care and treatment, current trends in the sport, and rules and regulations.

You can read straight through or skip around. But no matter how and when you get it, all the information is vital. In some states, for example, it is permissible to take a young bird from its nest, but to do this you must know not only your state law but also the nesting habits of the bird. In other states, only adult birds may be taken. This poses another special problem which is covered in the trapping section.

So let's get started on the first steps toward happy hunting!

3

The Language
of Falconry

Accipiter — a short-winged hawk.

Austringer — a falconer who trains and hunts accipiters.

Bate — to fly wildly off the glove or perch.

Bewit — a small leather strap used to fasten a bell to a hawk.

Bind — when a hawk seizes its prey in the air or on the ground.

Block — a wooden block used for a falcon's perch.

Braces — leather thongs which open and close a hawk hood.

Brail — a leather thong used to bind a hawk's wing.

Brancher — a young hawk that has left the nest but still remains in vicinity.

Buteo — the Latin name for slow-flying, circling hawks (for example, Red-Tailed).

Cadge — a rectangular perch for hawks carried in the field.

Cadger — one who carries the cadge.

Call off — to call a hawk to the falconer, from a perch or another glove.

Carry — to attempt to fly off with meat or quarry at falconer's approach.

Cast — two falcons flying together, or . . . the act of regurgitating a pellet, or . . . to hold a hawk so that it cannot move.

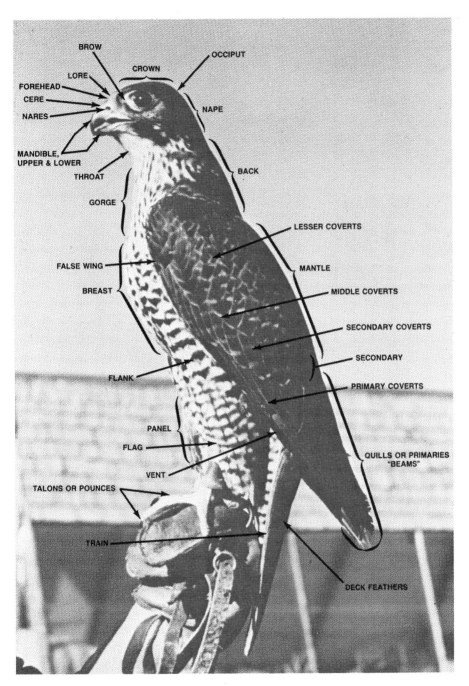

The parts of a hawk

Casting — the pellet of undigested fur, bones, or feathers regurgitated through the mouth by a hawk.

Cere — the yellow, waxlike skin above the beak.

Check — to leave one quarry and chase another.

Cope — to cut back the beak or talons of a hawk.

Crabbing — two falcons fighting.

Creance — a long line (usually nylon monofilament today) used to tether hawks while flying them in training.

Crop — the pouch just above the breastbone in hawks. Used to store food before it passes into the stomach.

Deck feathers — the two central tail feathers.

Eyass, Eyas — young hawk either still in nest or trained after being taken from nest.

Eyrie, Aerie, Eyry — ledge of a falcon nest on a cliff.

Falcon — one of the long-winged hawks. Also the female of the long-winged hawks.

Feak — when a hawk wipes its beak on its perch after eating.

Foot — to successfully bind to or catch its quarry.

Frounce — a disease of the throat and mouth of hawks.

Get in — approach a hawk after it has made a kill.

Gorge — a hawk eating all it can.

Hack — a state of flying free, usually referring to young hawks that are allowed to fly free after they have learned to fly for a few weeks.

Haggard — adult hawks that have been trapped.

Hood — a leather cap used to blind hawks to light.

Hunger Traces (also called shock traces) — white marks in tail feathers, caused by hunger or shock.

Imping — repairing broken flight feathers.

Intermewed — a hawk that has moulted in confinement.

Jack — the male of the Pigeon Hawk or Merlin.

Jerkin — the male of the Gyrfalcon.

Jesses — strips of leather that are permanently attached to the legs of a hawk.

Jonk — to sleep.

Leash — a length of leather thong used to fasten a hawk's jesses to its perch.

Lure — a leather object to which falconer may fasten feathers or fur and to which is tied meat. For training hawks to attack.

Make in — to move in to a hawk with its quarry on ground.

Man — to handle, to gentle a hawk.

Mantle — to stretch out a leg and a wing simultaneously.

Mew — the room in which hawks are kept, or . . . to moult.

Mutes — the excrement of hawks.

Panel — the stomach of a hawk.

Passage hawk — a hawk that is captured on migration.

Penned-hard — when the shafts of the flight feathers have hardened . . . ready for flight.

Pitch — the altitude a hawk reaches while "waiting on" for the flush of game.

Plume — pull off feathers.

Point — rise over the spot where quarry has avoided capture.

Pounces — talons.

Preen — arrange its own feathers.

Put in — Falcon driving quarry to cover.

Put out — falconer driving quarry out in open for hawk.

Put up — rise and hover over quarry.

Rake out — fly too wide of the falconer.

Ramage — wild.

Rangle — small stones given to hawks to aid crop and digestion.

Ring — flying up in a spiral.

Rouse — shaking its feathers.

Rufter hood — an easy-fitting hood used for hawks when first captured.

Sails — the wings of a hawk.

Serve — give a hawk an opportunity to catch game.

Soar — ride the thermals.

Stoop — dive upon the quarry.

Take the air — rise high in the air to escape falcon.

Tiercel — the male of any hawk used in falconry.

Tiring — tough pieces of meat or bone given to a hawk for exercises.

Train — the tail of a hawk . . . also a live quarry given to a hawk.

Truss — "bind to" or seize quarry.

Varvels — small rings fastened to the end of jesses.

Wait on — hover or fly above the falconer.

Weathering — placing hawks out in good weather.

Yarak — a Turkish term meaning an accipiter is ready for hunting.

4

The Equipment

I APPRECIATE HOW eager you may be to get on with the fun of flying your hunting hawk, but don't let this chapter on falconry equipment turn you off. If you really can't wait to get into the more exciting aspects of the sport, just skim through this material and come back to it later before you are ready to get your bird. Just remember that when you set out to capture or purchase a hunting bird, you must have the proper equipment ready for it.

Falconry equipment is so traditionally complicated that a newcomer may get the impression that the gear of the "ancient and noble art" is not only too hard to come by but also too expensive. Cheer up. A beginner can make every piece of equipment needed, except perhaps the fine bells fastened to the hawk's legs and the swivels, although since swivels can be purchased in any good fishing-tackle store, there is hardly any need to make them.

For those who prefer to buy their gear ready-made, a list of manufacturers appears at the end of this chapter. The equipment is far from inexpensive, especially bags and hoods, but it might pay to buy one

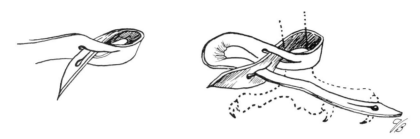

Traditional jesses and how they are attached to hawk's foot (dotted line).

or two good hoods in order to take them apart to fashion your own patterns.

The making of jesses, leashes, hoods, perches, cadges, gloves, lures, traps, patterns, and falconers' bags, plus the tying of all the knots, is relatively simple. You might have some difficulty finding the exact fit of a hood for your hawk, but even this problem is not too difficult to solve.

The first piece of equipment you should attempt to make is a set of conventional leather jesses. It is difficult to pinpoint the weight of leather you need for these, so let's just say you want leather about the thickness of a good leather jacket or a pair of heavy leather work gloves.

This is the first piece of equipment (with the possible exception of a soft hood) to put on a hawk that has just been captured. Note the illustrations of the traditional jess and the Aylmeri jess.

The leather should be laid flat on a wooden cutting board and cut out slowly and carefully with a cutting razor or modeler's knife. In making the three slits in the jess, first make a clean, small hole with a nail punch and start the slit from there. This will prevent the slit from lengthening and the leather from splitting under strain.

I found out the hard way (by losing a hawk as a youngster) that jesses must be soaked or periodically rubbed with oil, a light, clear, nondetergent oil of any kind, such as a neat's-foot oil. If this is not done, the hawk can pick away at a dried-out jess, eventually cutting through

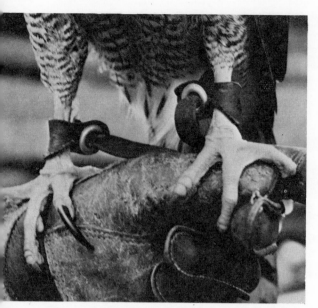

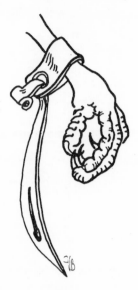

Falcon fitted with Aylmeri jesses.

*Detail of Aylmeri jess
on falcon's foot.*

with its sharp beak. A hawk cannot cut through an oiled jess or leash, because it is too slippery and resilient.

I make all my jesses with two sections (see drawing) joined by a good stainless-steel ballbearing swivel of the kind used for saltwater game fish (see photo). This arrangement is to prevent the jesses from becoming entangled when the hawk turns around several times on its perch or when it falls off, hangs, then flies back up. Tying the jess to the leg is simple, but you should practice doing it several times beforehand by substituting a large pencil for the hawk leg.

The length is up to the individual falconer. Obviously the shorter the jess, the less chance it has of hanging up the bird in the wild. I suggest from six inches for a sparrow hawk to eight or nine inches for the

Jess rigged with swivel.

Snap swivels and rotating swivels for jess attachment.

larger hawks. The leash connecting the ends of the two jesses and then leading to the screen porch should be several feet long, varying to suit each falconer.

The knurl knot at the end of the leather leash (see drawing) is an important knot because it is virtually impossible to have it pull out and will last a long time. Here again, it is important to keep the leash and knurl knot oiled since sunlight and water can cause them to crack, rot, and break. The making and the size of the small leather bewit — for fastening bells to hawks' legs — is made clear by an accompanying drawing.

Along with the jesses and leash, I would have ready in advance a soft hood. I carry at least three sizes while looking for migrating hawks.

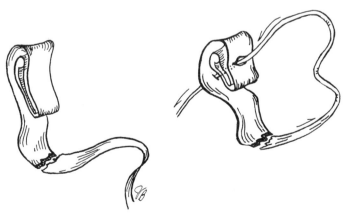

Knurl knot, made as shown, forms "button" on leash end.

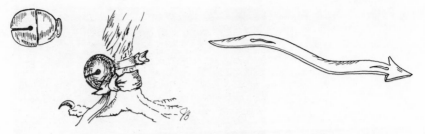

Bewit, cut to this pattern, holds bell to hawk's leg.

You never know what size hawk will be taken. The basic pattern (see drawing) is an Indian style I have used since the 1940s. I don't even remember where I got it. I usually make it from soft leather with loose and pliable drawstrings to fit through slits at the back. We sewed these by hand and then turned them inside out. But with today's rapid-drying epoxy-type glues, it's quicker to glue these Indian- and Dutch-style hoods together. (A plume can be mounted on the top where the drawings show an X, but it is merely ornamental and not necessary.) The photo shows typical Indian and Dutch hoods.

Since you will be bringing the newly acquired hawk home to its first mew or darkened room, you must have the screen perch (see drawing) ready. It is simple to build. Just make sure that it is sturdy enough to remain standing when a hawk bates (flies wildly from the padded top

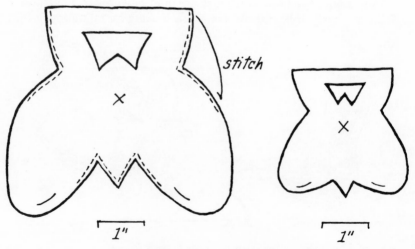

Size of hood pattern varies to suit need.

Back row: wood and metal forms for shaping leather hoods. Front row: examples of completed hoods.

bar or perch) and hits the end of the leash. By making the screen perch four-legged, you can achieve this stability. Many times an old table from a junk shop can be used by taking off the top and making a screen perch out of it as shown. I would make it at least four feet high, because hawks become uneasy when anything that they fear might be an enemy can tower above them. Just think about the hawk in the wild where it

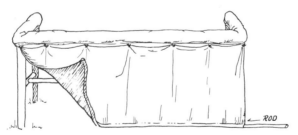

The screen perch must be ready when you bring your new hawk home.

The cadge, of historical interest, is something you probably won't need.

is most vulnerable from above. The canvas curtain, which hangs down and prevents the hawk from becoming tangled on the perch, should be weighted from the bottom. This can be done by attaching weights, such as lead fishing sinkers, or (as in this case) inserting a wooden rod through the base.

Now consider the cadge. A cadge was once used to carry several or more hawks in the field. I just show this for its nostalgic value in case anyone wanted to make one (see drawing). With today's mobility, one is hardly needed. Moreover, the modern falconer seldom flies more than one hawk at a time. The cadge was carried by a servant, sometimes an apprentice falconer who for obvious reasons was called a cadger.

The basic perches to be used later are shown in the accompanying drawings. I have lumped them into the old-style block perch, bow perch, T perch, and ring perch. The leather pieces (or, sometimes, wide rubber strips) shown on the ring perch prevent a hawk from passing through the ring and shortening its leash. The same straps should be used on the bow perch, although they are not illustrated here.

All these perches usually have been made from wood — even the ring perch, which can be made by bending green branches and lashing them together. However, more and more hawk furniture is being made in a blacksmith shop or garage and lasts a lot longer. The main shafts of the perches should be made of metal, if possible, and thrust deeply into the ground. A large hawk or eagle is very powerful and can yank a perch from the soft earth with ease once it becomes loose. I have had a hawk hop off with a perch and travel dozens of yards before getting hung up on some obstacle.

In general, the block perches are used for the bigger falcons because they spend most of their lives standing and nesting on rock ledges. It is not necessary to pad a block perch for a prairie falcon or a gyrfalcon.

Left to right: block perch, bow perch, T perch. Bow perch needs crosspieces for completion.

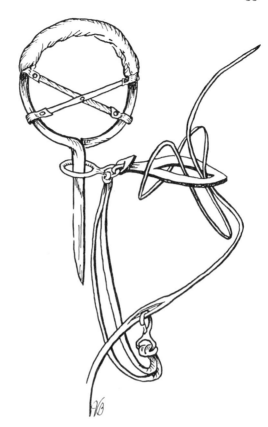

Ring perch (note cross-pieces) and falconer's knot.

They have huge feet and literally stand flat-footed on perches. Lately some falconers have nailed wire mesh to these perches and topped them with cement. The bow, T, and ring perches are used for several of the smaller falcons and the accipiters, all perching hawks accustomed to trees.

The other item indispensable for all perches is the iron or steel ring that slides up and down the main shaft or one leg of the perch. This should be heavy, not as flimsy as a hollow, brass curtain-rod ring. It must withstand shock and not be weakened by rust. Any good hardware store carries suitable rings.

The top of a bow, T, or ring perch should be wrapped with canvas or some other rough material to help the hawk get a firm grip. This is particularly important in the first few months of its captivity. You don't want a newly captured hawk constantly slipping off a slick wooden

This variation of bow perch has a doormat grip for accipiters.

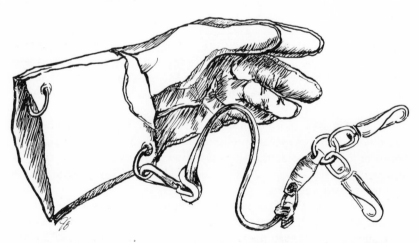

You can buy a falconer's glove or rig your own from a welder's glove.

perch. A metal perch certainly needs to be padded. The cold metal is bad for a hawk under any circumstances.

Falconer's gloves can be purchased, but I see nothing wrong with using a welder's leather glove. It is thick enough to prevent all but eagles from piercing it with talons. A glove with the rough side of the leather out gives the hawk a better foothold. Rings should be attached to the glove as shown, using the short hunting leash with a revolving ball-bearing swivel and two snaps. I like the two snaps. If the metal spring on one breaks in the field, you have the insurance of the second.

The all-important lure can be made in several ways. Some falconers who like to make it as much like a wild game bird as possible tie such things as pigeon wings, rabbit fur, or duck breast feathers to the leather lure. I have found that a simple leather lure, no matter what its color, is enough to bring a hawk back to the falconer. I do prefer, however, the rotating leather lure (see drawing) because it simulates the flapping of wings of a wild bird.

A falconer needs this piece of equipment whenever he is in the field with his hawk. Since the hawk has been taught that you, its master, are the source of its food, this is the only reason a hawk will return to you.

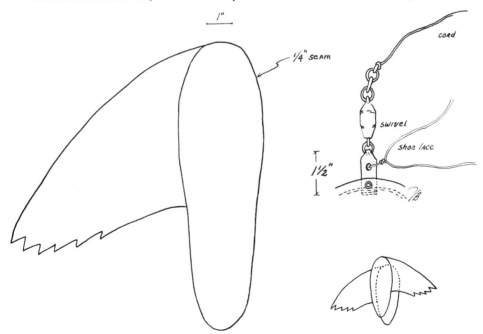

Whenever you are in the field with your hawk, you need to carry a rotating lure. You can increase lure's weight by adding sand.

To make a lure too heavy is to ask for injury to the hawk when it strikes it in mid air as it should. If a lure is too light in the initial training stages, particularly with young birds, the hawk will sometimes try to fly off with it after fastening to it.

As a rule of thumb, I suggest the lure be too light rather than too heavy. Filling leather with a bit of sand gives it sufficient weight yet does not make it too hard. A few ounces is enough for the smaller hawks and certainly no more than eight ounces for the bigger ones.

Since the leather lure can be washed off periodically, it doesn't become as smelly as bird wings with chunks of meat tied to them each day. Several shoelaces (which can be changed every so often) should be fastened to the lure near the head (see drawing detail) so several chunks of beef can be tied with them. The lure is fastened by a strong saltwater ball-bearing swivel to about 12 to 15 feet of heavy cord. This should be strong cord of a bright color because occasionally the lure is dropped in grass and it can be spotted better. I prefer a leather lure of bright yellow alternated with some other color. The cord is fastened to a piece of wood about eight inches long. A sawed-off piece of broom handle will do. The cord is wrapped around this and carried in the falconer's bag when not used. Sharpen one end of this piece of wood so that as you put it aside when working with a hawk you can anchor it by thrusting it into the ground.

This leather rotating lure has wings of contrasting colors. Note assortment of hoods.

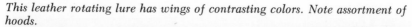

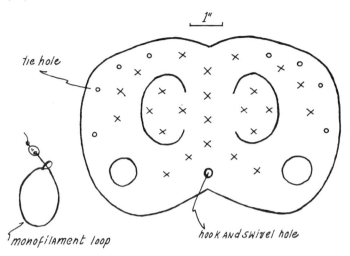

Pattern of pigeon harness, drawn to scale. Detail shows how to rig loop with glass bead.

Another piece of equipment is the harness to fit over a live pigeon. Follow the size indicated in the inch scale. The harness can be a third to a half smaller for starlings. The X's mark where nylon or monofilament fishing-line loops are fastened. For a starling harness to be used with smaller hawks, use mono as light as 2-pound-test. I would use 6- to 8-pound loops for Cooper's hawks and 12-pound loops for anything bigger. I don't think the loop need be bigger than 1½ to 2 inches, the smaller better than the larger.

The secret for keeping the loops from pulling out of the holes in the leather is to fasten them inside to a small glass bead. A small rubber shock absorber fastened to the back of the lure at the hook-and-swivel hole will prevent a fast-moving hawk from snapping the 15-foot nylon cord attached to the harness. A piece of wood — a 6-inch dowel is enough — should be tied to the end of the cord and the cord or nylon line (at least 25-pound test) wound upon it. As for the weight of the harness or the thickness of the leather, I suggest it be made out of the rough leather of a welder's glove. This gives it about the right weight and strength. The loops won't pull out, and the weight will help keep the hawk from flying off with the dead pigeon or starling plus the harness. Of course the 15 feet of 25-pound-test nylon and the dowel won't let it get very far. But there is no use in underestimating the strength of hawks.

The last item needed is a falconer's bag. You can purchase one that is beautifully made. But basically all you need is a leather or canvas bag

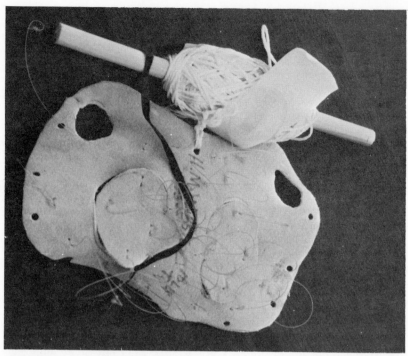

Close-up of pigeon harness rigged with monofilament loops, rubber shock absorber, and coiled line.

Falconer's bag carries lure in one compartment. Other compartment carries meat to feed hawk in order to get it back to lure.

Modern tracking equipment for lost hawks includes radio receiver, earphones, and antenna.

with two main compartments — one for the lure, and the other for meat with which to feed the hawk in order to get it back to the lure. Killed game can be stored in the bag, too, so the bigger the better. It should be hung from a strap, and a swivel should be used between the carrying strap and the bag so it can be switched from side to side in the field. The main thing is that the meat side should have a removable lining (much like today's trout creels that snap in and out of a fishing jacket) so that it can be cleaned and aired regularly.

Nowadays, radiotelemetry plays a part in falconry. It's not difficult to understand why.

In the old days, hawks were flown in areas of wide-open spaces, free of distractions. Lost hawks were not a big problem. And because there was no scarcity of hawks, a falconer was not so worried about losing a hawk as one would be today.

But today, with hawks hard to get, a falconer wants to be absolutely certain that if a bird gets away it will be recovered. So today's falcon — when being flown at game — may be equipped with a tiny radio transmitter fastened to a leg. If the bird strays, the falconer may have

Accurate device for weighing your hawk is a postage scale like this one or a counter-balance scale. With either, be sure to allow for the weight of the perch.

to depend upon a radio signal transmitted across a range of about eight miles. The signal will continue for about two weeks, until the tiny batteries die down.

Meantime, the falconer — equipped with headphones, antenna, and radio receiver — goes afield and rotates his directional antenna until he picks up the sound of radio transmission. Then he follows the sound in that direction until he locates the lost hawk.

Among the most important items in falconry is the weighing scale. There are two types that can be used.

One is the postage-type scale calibrated in ¼-ounce increments for small hawks or ½-ounce steps for the larger birds. The flat weighing pan may be removed and a wooden perch substituted so that the hawk can find a grip when perching.

The other type of weighing scale, and perhaps more accurate type, is the counter-balance design. But the perch arrangement should be the same as the one just described.

Equipped with this paraphernalia, the novice falconer is ready for any hawk.

For the benefit of the beginner who does not want to make gear but would rather buy it already made, the following is a list of manufacturers in this country, Canada, Europe, and Asia.

U.S.A. Pete Asborno, 4530 West 31st Avenue, Denver, Colorado, 80212 — bells; H. Eugene Johnson, 2344 Nomad Avenue, Dayton, Ohio, 45414 — hoods; Kalen Glove Manufactury, 2557 North Dubonnet Avenue, Rosemead, California, 91770 — gloves and other equipment.

Canada. Lloyd Cook, 1024 McGregor Avenue, Victoria, British Columbia — lure with flapping wings.

Europe. R.C. Upton, The Leather Shop, 78 High Street, Marlborough, England; M. J. Dawson, 99 Eldred Avenue, Brighton, Sussex, England — agent for Dutch-made equipment, the hoods being made from original blocks of famous Dutch falconer Adriaan Mollen; A. Gates, Ken-Dor, Oak Walk, St. Peter, Jersey, England — Aylmeri jesses.

Asia. Ch. Mohammed Din & Co., Prem Gali No. 4, Railway Road, Lahore, Pakistan.

If these sources do not prove satisfactory, contact the North American Falconers Association, Post Office Box 1484, Denver, Colorado, 80201; The Falconry Centre, Newent, Gloucester, England; or the Canadian Raptor Society, Box 37, Saanichton, B.C., Canada.

5

The Hunting Hawks
of North America

MOST EUROPEAN FALCONRY books are full of terms that do not
relate to North American hawks. Most British books (more have been
published in England than anywhere else) divide hunting birds of prey
into two distinct classes: the true long-winged falcons, and the accipiters
(short-winged hawks).

Some names crop up constantly to confuse the neophyte American
falconer: saker, merlin, tiercel, lanner, sparrow hawk, kestrel. The saker
and lanner are desert falcons found in the Middle East and brought
to Europe by falconers who first learned of them from the Crusaders.
They are comparable to our Western prairie falcon, but you will never
see one in North America unless it has escaped from some hapless falconer who paid an arm and a leg for it.

The tiercel is simply the smaller male of the peregrine and the goshawk, about a third smaller than the female. The merlin, a true small
falcon of Europe, can be compared to our pigeon hawk. Feeding almost
exclusively on songbirds, the pigeon hawk was one of the first to be hard
hit by DDT. I have seen many in the Rocky Mountain states the past
few years.

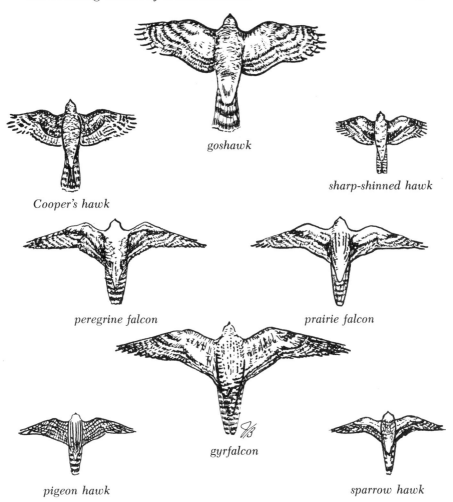

goshawk

Cooper's hawk

sharp-shinned hawk

peregrine falcon

prairie falcon

gyrfalcon

pigeon hawk

sparrow hawk

Identifying Hawks in Flight

The sparrow hawk in Europe is what we call the sharp-shinned hawk, the smallest species of our accipiter hawks (although the females can be as big as our male Cooper's hawks). The Europeans call our sparrow hawk the kestrel, but they refer only to the much bigger female, considered unfit as a falcon in olden days when only "knaves" were allowed to own them. I know many Americans who own female sparrow hawks and enjoy them. These hawks won't kill anything much bigger than a starling, but they have a great disposition and make an affectionate pet and a fairly good hunting hawk if you don't demand too much.

Just remember that your sparrow hawk may be just as interested in swooping down to pick up a juicy grasshopper as in catching an English sparrow or a cowbird.

I encourage novice falconers to start out with a sparrow hawk, not for hunting, but just to become familiar with the mannerisms of falcons. They are regal, independent, beautifully colored, and trim little birds who reward careful training with a measure of devotion.

My youngest son, Jim, and I have trapped and spent many a happy hour with the sleek little sparrow hawks. Though we never had any startling success in hunting them, we have grown fond of a number of them. They can be taught to fly to the wrist from quite a distance, and they have the same configuration as the larger peregrines and gyrfalcons.

The owls also make interesting pets. But unless you are equipped with infrared eyeballs, you won't be hunting any. I raised the great-horned, the barred, the barn, and the long-eared owls and found them interesting. But I shall never forget the night years ago when a great-horned owl broke a leash after we put all the birds to rest on the floor of a bird-of-prey house at the Trailside Museum and turned the lights out. The next morning we found that the great-horned owl had systematically killed a peregrine falcon, a broad-winged hawk, a red-shouldered hawk, a female Cooper's hawk, two sharp-shinned hawks, several sparrow hawks, and even a barn owl. It had eaten none of its victims.

A new falconer introduces his sparrow hawk to a new area.

The great-horned owl makes an interesting pet but will hunt only at night.

Other hawks fall into the class of the broad-winged hawks, including the red-tailed, the red-shouldered, the broad-winged, the Harris, the rough-legged, and even the harriers, such as the marsh hawk. These hawks — all of which I have captured and raised — make interesting pets. But hunting hawks they are not. They can be taught to fly to the wrist, they are spectacular to watch, and they are fun to raise and train. Jim kept an injured red-tailed hawk until its wing healed, and he turned it loose in the spring. It was a fine hawk and became quite tame. It might possibly have hunted small game if we had wanted to work at it, but it was a pleasant, gentle hawk that subsisted on a diet of mice and hamburger for eight months and returned to the wild as it had left it. We have always hoped it didn't glide down and try to land on the wrist of

The red-tailed hawk is fine as a pet but has little ability as a hunter.   *The red-shouldered hawk won't hunt much except rodents.*

a duck hunter in a blind or approach a hunter looking for grouse. There might have been a wide communication gap there.

Skip the osprey, even as a pet. I raised three of them. They are not a particularly bright bird and will spend the entire time "peeping" for food (fish) long after they have become adults. Beautiful on the wing and in the wild, they are clumsy and absurd in captivity. I doubt if anyone ever taught one how to catch even a carp, not that this would be hard. It's just not very interesting.

And let me emphasize that you must stay away from the endangered species such as the peregrine falcon and the bald and golden eagles, all of which are protected by federal and state laws.

For practical purposes you will be looking for one of seven species of hawks—four falcons and three accipiters. These are: in the falcon family—an arctic gyrfalcon, a prairie falcon, a pigeon hawk, and a tiny sparrow hawk; in the accipiter or short-winged class—the goshawk, the Cooper's hawk, and the sharp-shinned hawk.

Since one of the first steps in obtaining a hawk in the wild is locating a nest, you need a knowledge of the hawks' characteristics, particularly their range, habitats, field marks, and such. The females are generally preferred because they are at least a third larger than the males. (This does not rule out the male. I had several male peregrines many years ago and a male Cooper's hawk which was as fierce as a hunting hawk can get.)

There are conflicting opinions about which sex makes the better hunter. It has been my experience that the large female haggard hawks trapped in the wild make by far the best hunters when finally taught not to fear the falconer. These fine birds have learned their hunting and killing trade well from wild parents and do not need to be taught by a falconer. The same is generally true of the passager hawk — the young adult. But what you get on the credit side with the wild adult birds is counterbalanced by their natural desire to escape and revert to the wild. By contrast, the nestlings can be raised to almost trust the human and to make really good pets occasionally. But they must be patiently taught how to hunt — first by use of the lure, and later by introducing them to live birds. Their chances of taking off for the wilds are much slimmer

A contrasting character is the peregrine falcon, shown here on the block.

than the adults', but there is no question in my mind that a young nest-ling bird taught to hunt by a falconer never quite achieves the verve and style of a hunting falcon or accipiter taught in the wild.

Following are detailed descriptions of the birds suited for the sport of falconry.

The gyrfalcons. This group (*Falco rusticolus*) consists of four falcons — all extremely northern and all of a slightly different color phase. All the gyrfalcons are big hawks — with a length of almost two feet for the females and a few inches shorter for the tiercels (males). The wingspread can go from 50 to 55 inches, and the color can range from pure white in the Greenland gyrfalcon to a dark slate-gray in the black gyrfalcon.

• The white gyrfalcon is also known as the Greenland gyrfalcon. It is sometimes seen in the extreme northeast corner of New England.

The magnificent white gyrfalcon is a superb hunting hawk.

• The gray gyrfalcon differs from the white gyrfalcon only in the slight shade of coloration. Its range is almost the same as that of the white gyrfalcon — the Arctic from Alaska east to Greenland, and in the winter a casual visitor might be seen as far south as Kansas, Wisconsin, Ontario, Maine, and New Hampshire.

• The MacFarlane's gyrfalcon is slightly smaller than the white gyrfalcon, but for our purposes it is still the same bird. Its head is unstreaked, and the underparts are white and heavily streaked with grayish-brown. But here again, only an ornithologist could really be too concerned about the difference. The range is about the same as the white and gray and it will seldom be found south of Minnesota, New York, Massachusetts, and Maine.

• The black gyrfalcon is simply darker than the others and has the same general range.

All four gyrfalcons are true falcons and can be found nesting only in the Arctic. Their nests are usually on cliffs or on the tundra and are composed of sticks, seaweed, and any other material which happens to be handy. Two to four eggs are usually laid. They are heavily spotted with varying shades of reddish-brown. Egg collecting (which was a popular hobby decades ago) should be highly discouraged.

I'll tell you about methods of trapping the gyrfalcon shortly. Just keep in mind that the same system should be used to capture these big hawks that is used on the prairie falcon and the goshawk, biggest of the accipiters. They are fast, tough, and mean. A lot is needed to hold them.

The prairie falcon. The prairie falcon (*Falco mexicanus Schlegel*) is spectacular and fairly common. It lives in the West, in arid and non-agricultural areas. For this reason, the prairie falcon was spared the fate of the peregrine and the pigeon hawk, which were hit hard by pesticides in the heavily populated and agricultural East and Midwest. The prairie falcon nests on cliffs, much like the peregrine (duck hawk), and feeds primarily on birds and small rodents. It can be found from the eastern border of the Great Plains and from southern British Columbia and southeastern Saskatchewan to lower California and southern Mexico. It can also be found as a casual visitor in all the states from there to Minnesota and the Mississippi River. The prairie falcon usually lays from two to five eggs, creamy-white and covered with spots and streaks of brown.

The pigeon hawk. With a little bit of luck, the beginner might find the magnificent, chunky, and sociable pigeon hawk (*Falco columbarius Linnaeus*). Called a merlin in Europe, this bird has been hard hit by pesticides since it follows the yearly migration of small songbirds, in much the same way as the sharp-shinned hawk. The pigeon hawk nests

*A hooded prairie falcon on
the fist.*

on ledges or in the branches of trees or occasionally, like the sparrow hawk, in the holes in hollow trees vacated by flickers and owls. It is not much bigger than the female sparrow hawk, and the only difference to the novice will be that it appears as a darker small falcon. It has a wide range—from northwestern Alaska (where it breeds across the northern tier of Canadian provinces to Ungava Bay) to the western, southwestern, midwestern and eastern states as far south as Mexico, Central America, and the West Indies in the winter.

The sparrow hawk. Some falconers claim the sparrow hawk (*Falco sparverius Linnaeus*), commonly called the kestrel in Europe, is hardly worthwhile fooling with. But it is a joy to raise and can become a fairly proficient hunting hawk provided you get a large female. The smaller, brightly colored males are a delight just to watch, but they will rarely kill anything bigger than a sparrow. But that hardly matters. They are true falcons, and you may learn much about the habits of these great birds from watching even the smallest of them. Sparrow hawks nest just about anywhere — from hollow trees to the eaves of houses and barns — and are found in just about every state in the United States and Canada. They winter as far south as Mexico, Florida, and the West Indies.

The goshawk. The biggest of the accipiters (short-winged hawks) is the magnificent goshawk (*Accipiter gentilis*). It is as large as the gyrfalcon. The females reach two feet in length and the males not much smaller. The goshawk attains a wingspread of almost 50 inches and is perhaps the fiercest hawk in the world. Unlike the falcons, this bird — like its two smaller relatives, the Cooper's and sharp-shinned hawks — kills by going directly after its prey. It does not hunt with the graceful high-circling moves of a falcon which climbs above its prey and dives upon it. I have seen goshawks fly right through bushes in pursuit of a

With luck, beginner might acquire a pigeon hawk.

Female sparrow hawk can become a fairly proficient hunter.

The big and magnificent goshawk grows to barely tolerate the falconer.

pheasant or rabbit. They are somewhat battered as a result, but no less ferocious. Goshawks grow to barely tolerate their master, the falconer, while I feel the falcons actually seem to develop a fondness for their trainers.

The accipiter is a slugger and a brawler and likes nothing better than to catch sight of a fleeing quarry. The hunting habits of most accipiters lack style, but I enjoy hunting them just as much as I do the falcons. I think it is the sheer abandon with which accipiters go after the game that appeals to me. I have not found them hard to train. They are unafraid of humans and will quickly adjust to captivity — if never really getting to like it.

Most of these big hawks nest in conifers at a considerable altitude. The nests are hard to spot, taking considerable looking with a good pair of binoculars. The nest is usually close to the trunk of the tree and on a sturdy branch or two. These short-winged hawks are not creatures of the open field. If you want to find one, you must haunt the heavy woodlots and thick timber. About the only time the novice will spot a goshawk, Cooper's, or sharp-shinned hawk is when it is flying swiftly through the thick trees with a series of rapid wing beats. If you are lucky, you will see one swoop up from close to the ground to a higher branch near the main trunk of a tree. It is among the most elusive of all the hawks.

The Cooper's hawk. This hawk (*Accipiter cooperii*) is really a small version of the goshawk, and the sharp-shinned hawk is just a small version of the Cooper's. The difficulty with identifying these hawks is that the male of the goshawk is about the same size as the female of the Cooper's and the female sharp-shinned is pretty close to the size of the small male Cooper's. They all have the same configuration, and the young look much like the males. Unless you are a fine ornithologist, it is difficult to tell the difference.

The Cooper's hawk is a fair-sized bird — about 20 inches in length (female) and with a wingspan of about 36 inches. Like the goshawk and the sharp-shinned hawk, the bird flies with a series of quick wing beats and a glide. Like most of the accipiters, the adult is liable to have a ferocious-looking, orange-reddish eye — a real calling card.

The secret of finding its nest is to look for a large field or open park in an otherwise wooded area and work in from there. Usually the nest will be not more than 100 yards in from the open space. Hawks are not lazy, just smart. There is no point in flying more than necessary. The Cooper's hawks nest in tall trees, sometimes using an old crow's nest or some other hawk's nest. One of the secrets of spotting hawks' nests is to look for a flat platform of sticks — always in a solid crotch. What dif-

The Cooper's hawk looks like a small version of goshawk.

ferentiates a hawk's nest from a squirrel's is the absence of leaves in the
hawk nest.

Depending upon the section of the country, most hawks lay their
eggs in May or June. The best way to find hawks' nests is to search for
them in the winter months and mark the bole of the tree with a paint
spot when there are no leaves above to obscure the nest. Then, using a
map made in the winter, go back in the spring and look under the tree
for "whitewash" (hawk droppings), pellets (which are regurgitated oblong
cylinders of either fur or feathers mixed with bits of bone), or bones
from the food dropped over the edge of the nests by the young.

The Cooper's hawk breeds from southern British Columbia and
southern Alberta across the northern tier of states, including Colorado,
Nebraska, Ohio, and New England, and winters as far south as Costa
Rica.

All these accipiters go by such local names as blue hen hawk, blue
chicken hawk, blue darter, partridge hawk, quail hawk, chicken hawk,
bullet hawk, striker, and others.

The sharp-shinned hawk. The sharp-shinned hawk (*Accipiter striatus velox*) is the smallest of the accipiters. It is a mean little critter and as ferocious for its size as its bigger cousin, the goshawk. It will readily attack anything its own size. A large female makes a formidable hunting hawk. The smaller male is a bit light, but it makes up in nervousness and a fierce disposition what it lacks in size. My experiences with all the accipiters is that they have one outstanding redeeming feature: they are afraid of little — including man — and it is relatively easy to train them. Unlike some of the more wary falcons, they hunt for the sheer joy of the kill.

The little sharp-shinned hawk usually nests in a coniferous tree of some sort, close to the bole and fairly high up. The nest is hard to spot. These hawks are secretive about allowing anyone to see them fly to it, usually flying to other trees in the vicinity with prey for the young and making sure no one is around before flying directly to the nest. Incidentally, if a novice should find an accipiter nest, it is wise, when climbing up to it, to wear a football helmet, a baseball mask, or a fencing mask. The bigger accipiters will dive straight for your face and head, and I have seen some nasty scratches from their talons. (The falcons, on

The sharp-shinned hawk, when in the wild, eats mainly songbirds.

the other hand, seldom display this disregard for their own safety.) The eggs of the sharp-shinned hawk are usually four or five in number and a dull bluish- or greenish-white.

This hawk breeds just about anywhere in the northern United States and winters all the way to Panama. Like the pigeon hawk, it follows closely the yearly migration of songbirds and eats birds almost exclusively.

Even though the great peregrine falcon (*Falco peregrinus anatum bonaparte*) is protected, it deserves mention as perhaps the greatest hunting falcon on the North American continent. I raised and hunted four many years ago. The first two, taken from nests on Storm King Moun-

The protected peregrine is perhaps North America's greatest hunting falcon.

tain near West Point, New York, in the late 1930s, were exceptional pets as well as hunters. The last two were captured in the late 1940s and early 1950s as grown-up (haggard) hawks and live-trapped while on migration. I kept them only a short time, hunted them both successfully, then released them to the wild. I am sorry now I freed them, since both probably died of pesticide poisoning.

The peregrine is a large falcon. The female is about 19 inches long, the male somewhat smaller, perhaps 17 inches. The wingspread is 40 to 46 inches. The bird is a spectacular aerial performer. Near the cliffs of Storm King Mountain, above the Hudson River, we once used a stopwatch to estimate a peregrine's killing dive, or "stoop," at between 100 and 120 miles per hour. I believe it may have been faster but had no way of proving it scientifically. We released healthy pigeons from a trap near the cliff and watched peregrines dive and kill them during the nesting season. I can still hear the sound of their dives as they pulled out of that descent, wings almost completely folded. As they passed overhead at full speed the sound resembled a quick tearing of paper. They hit the pigeons at full speed and then casually circled around and picked up their quarry as it fell. The sound of the contact came back to us as a sharp cracking sound, echoing against the towering sheer cliff walls.

The peregrine breeding range was (and still is to a limited extent) from Alaska on the west to Greenland on the east (nesting grounds) and their wintering range from lower California to the eastern seaboard where they were occasionally found as far south as the West Indies, Panama, and South America.

There is a concerted effort to reestablish this great bird to the wilds today. I hope the attempt will succeed. In the meantime, many are being raised in captivity, so the species is in little danger of extinction. Perhaps someday the peregrine will reappear in sufficient numbers to be included in our list of available hunting hawks.

I won't dwell on the eagles, for two reasons. Both species, the bald and the golden, are protected, and the two I raised were too big and strong to consider as hunters. The bald was a scavenger, and the golden tried to tear off my ears and nose about once a day. Carrying him around on an arm, even with an extra-thick welding glove, was exhausting. And when he began to lose his balance and clamped down on my arm, it felt like a vise. Eagles can be raised to hunt, but it is a chore.

6

How to Get
Your Hawk

BE WARY OF advertisements placed by mail-order houses that sell hawks, eagles, owls, parakeets, monkeys, and so on. I looked into several of the biggest of these operations and found conditions appalling. The poor creatures, which had been imported, were crammed into cages far too small for them. Crippling and disease were rampant. Many of the creatures arrived dead at customs.

The mail-order houses sell for the fast buck, shipping only on receipt of money orders or certified checks. I know of three hawks — a Cooper's, a "lanner falcon" (which looked suspiciously like a bedraggled prairie falcon), and a male sparrow hawk — sent by a Florida mail-order house. They arrived dead from starvation and heat exhaustion. Moreover, many of the "foreign" hawks and eagles advertised by some mail-order firms were actually North American species illegally shipped across state lines.

There are sources, although not many, from which hawks can be purchased legally today. It is far better to try these sources than the mail-order houses. Most falconers' associations can tell the novice where birds can be bought, but at a high price.

One potential source is a person who obtained a hawk but decided not to develop into a successful falconer. Falconers' associations would more than likely get the word on these birds first. You also might see an ad for one in a local newspaper or in a few outdoor magazines. Word of mouth is another way of finding such birds, if you know a few professional falconers.

I used to become acquainted with poultry farmers, pigeon fanciers, and managers of game-bird farms and shooting preserves. These highly professional men each year trapped any number of hawks — mostly goshawks, great horned owls, and Cooper's hawks — which were harassing poultry and game birds. Usually they just wrung the necks of the hawks or owls and buried them. But they were also willing to turn one over to me at a price far lower than is commanded on the national and international markets today for an accipiter or falcon.

If there is any choice about the purchase of a hawk, I urge the novice to start with a hawk of a lower quality than he or she hopes eventually to end up with. If you hope to work with a regal gyrfalcon someday, start with the simple little sparrow hawk to learn the ways of falcons. If a big female goshawk is your ultimate aim, start with a modest sharp-shinned hawk, which will certainly hunt and also provide many insights into hawk behavior. If you are to make mistakes or lose a hawk, it is far better if you have a smaller and less-expensive or less-sophisticated bird.

A rule of thumb to follow in the purchase of a hunting hawk is that if you have access to plenty of room, such as a ranch or large farm, then a falcon — even the larger ones — will have space to maneuver. But if space in which to exercise and fly a hunting hawk is a problem, a better choice would be an accipiter. A goshawk, Cooper's, or sharp-shinned hawk needs little open space in which to hunt. I have seen them hunt successfully in brush and in thick timber. They don't require the room to circle above the quarry in order to dive "stoop." An accipiter usually follows directly after its prey, zig-zagging right behind it and smashing into thickets.

Rather than risk breaking a federal or state law, let's consider methods of obtaining hawks within the law. Remember, check your local state law. Some states require a scientific permit to obtain a hawk. I acquired such a federal permit — good also in several states — to do an article on falconry for *Field & Stream*. Not only should permits be granted to writers but also to students of ornithology or legitimate falconers as well. The federal and state agencies should be happy to award permits to responsible persons. If not, they should state why they refuse to do so.

The most rewarding way to get a hawk, of course, is to capture your own. This is why understanding the birds' nesting habits is so important. Getting to a nest — if you are fortunate enough to find one —

should involve common sense. When I think of the risks we novice falconers took going down the sheer face of Storm King Mountain, New
York, with ordinary ropes, dangling several hundred feet above the
railroad bed, I shudder. I would not do that today for a dozen white
gyrfalcons.

Today, few falconers will be lucky enough to find a falcon nest on
such a cliff. Getting to a tree nest involves fewer problems but still requires climbing skill — with ladders or pole-climbing spurs such as those
used by phone workers. An old method was to nail short steps into the
tree with large spikes as we went up, a heavy rope looped carefully
around both us and the tree. Again, in climbing to nests of the larger
two accipiters — which can do great damage with their talons — a crash
helmet, football helmet, catcher's mask, or fencing mask is advisable.

From here on, I shall deal with the wild trapping of hawks — those
which have just left the nest, or both young and adult birds on migration. We are concerned with the most efficient traps. Many have been
developed all over the world, but we can forget about a number of
them. They are too complicated, take up too much space, and weigh
too much. There are all sorts of noose traps set on collapsible poles
placed near poultry and game farms, but you almost have to live there
to tend the trap at all times. Since the captured bird hangs by one or
both legs in mid-air, suspended by a nylon monofilament fishing line,
there is always the danger of permanent injury. The bird can hang too
long and die in the sun, or it can become further entangled and strangle
itself. It can also break wings and legs if it is not taken from the trap
quickly.

The steel-jawed trap used to catch mink, muskrat, and fox is difficult for youngsters to obtain today. It is all well and good if used by a
commercial trapper who each day makes the rounds of his traps. When
I was a boy, we could purchase such traps cheaply in any hardware
store. They would be set atop a pole near farms or in open fields, the
steel jaws wrapped with cloth. We wired the traps so they snapped shut
only far enough to leave room for the leg of a hawk. They were efficient, but there are better methods today.

To catch a small sparrow hawk, the best system is to use a small
wire cage fitted all over with nooses of nylon fishing line and painted
black with spray paint to keep its shiny wire from reflecting light. Jim
and I have made many, from small ones about 1 foot square with sides
approximately 4 inches high with completely covered tops and bottoms,
to large ones 2 feet long and 18 inches wide. Rig as many nooses as you
can all over this type of trap. It is time consuming, but worth the effort.
Six-pound-test nylon monofilament will do for the small sparrow hawk

Practical small wire trap, spray-painted black and fitted with nylon loops, is baited with mouse. Trap catches sparrow hawks, sharp-shinned hawks, pigeon hawks, and occasionally Cooper's hawks.

and sharp-shinned hawk, but use 8-pound mono for Cooper's hawks and 12-pound mono for birds as large as prairie falcons and goshawks. The loops work better if the mono is slightly stiff. The loops down the sides can come in handy; I have seen a number of sparrow hawks lie on their sides and try to grab the small bird or mouse bait inside. Usually, however, since they will make their first attack from the top of the dome, that is where the most loops should be put.

This type of trap is quite old, probably made from woven reeds centuries ago. It is called a bal-chatri trap, probably because of its Indian origin. For the tiny hawks, any field mouse, white mouse, gerbil from a pet shop, English sparrow, or starling can be used as bait. (For going after the bigger buteos for banding, I have seen game-department personnel use hamsters, white rats, or — in the case of the accipiters — pigeons.) The bait, seldom touched by the hawks, can be used for months or years.

The trap with the bait inside is carried simply in a moving car in the trapper's lap. When a migrating hawk, a circling hawk, or a perching hawk is spotted, the car is slowed down, a door on the side of the car opposite from the hawk is opened, and the trap is dropped lightly just off the shoulder of the road or highway. The hawks do not associate the car with the trap if the dropping is done smoothly enough, although I have seen smart hawks (obviously trapped a number of times for band-

Female sparrow hawk caught in the nylon nooses of snare trap.

ing) take off as soon as they spot the trap. However, most hawks will stay and see the bait almost as soon as the car leaves it. I have seen sparrow hawks bob their heads several times and then dive on the trap almost immediately.

It is a good idea to speed up the car and travel some distance before slowing to a stop and turning around. The hawk can be watched with binoculars. As soon as you think it has been snared in the nooses, drive back to the trap. This is a fine method of taking all hawks. I am sure it would work just as well on the larger falcons, although I have never tried it on a gyrfalcon or goshawk.

Before you set out to catch a hawk, you must have the jesses and several pieces of equipment handy. A hawk which has just been trapped is frightened and angry. The tiny sparrow hawks can be held loosely and will not injure a hand if you are wearing a light-leather or heavy-cloth glove. But a welder's glove is necessary to deal with the larger hawks — particularly the goshawk and the bigger falcons, which can sink talons deep into a hand or arm. Soft, comfortable Indian-type hoods — in sizes to fit hawks expected to be in the area — should be available to slip over the bird's head as soon as possible. If the hawk can be hooded and rendered comfortable and immobile for a few moments, then soft jesses can be fastened to the legs. This procedure is recommended because in the first moments after capture, many a hawk has made a sudden break for freedom and gotten away through a car window or open door.

I worked out a practical technique by cutting from the calf area of women's nylon stockings foot-long sleeves which I carry stuffed into a shirt pocket. While a companion holds the newly captured hawk, I slip this sleeve down over the just-hooded hawk until it encases the entire body. The nylon sleeve does not harm the hawk, it keeps the feathers smooth, and it gives me time to get jesses on the bird without facing a lot of wing flapping. After hooding and fitting your hawk with jesses, the stocking may be slipped down and off. The hawk should be tied to something secure, where it will grip the perch automatically and not fall.

Another method of trapping, used in Asia and Europe for centuries and requiring little paraphernalia, is the net trap, or dho-gazza. Originally used in India, it consists of stakes placed in the ground in an L shape, with light mesh nets strung between them. These light nylon nets can be purchased at most fishing stores. The stakes should be about 7 feet long and the mesh of the net about 3 or 4 inches wide. The net and the stakes should be black, or at least a dark color, to make them as invisible as possible. Although a number of arrangements of these nets is

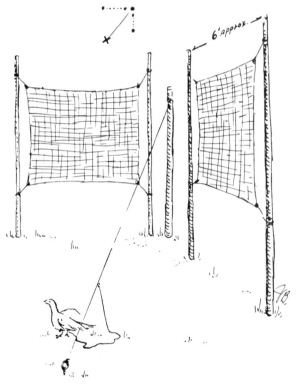

Idea behind dho-gazza trap is that diving and swooping hawks are supposed to get entangled in mesh.

possible, the operation is not complicated. A live tethered bird is placed between the two nets, and the diving and swooping hawks are supposed to be entangled in the nets. I have not had much luck with this method, but I know people who have.

Another tried-and-true trapping method is the dig-in. It is quite simple, but not practical where the ground is rocky or frozen. The falconer digs a pit, gets in, and covers it over, leaving outside a live pigeon tethered where it can be reached by hand. A sandy beach on a migration route is ideal for this system of trapping passage hawks. When the hawk grasps the bait, the falconer's hand can be inched through the sand until the bird is grasped by the legs.

There are all sorts of designs for Swedish traps, filled with pigeons. Primarily used for the capture of goshawks, they are permanent traps used near poultry and game farms.

Frank Beebe and Hal Webster, in their book *North American Falconry and Hunting Hawks,* describe a wire trap they call the noose carpet — a large chicken-wire oblong of about 2 feet by 3 feet, fitted with nooses and placed over a dead bird that has been killed by a hawk but left. This is useful if you are waiting for a bird to return to a kill. Beebe and Webster also describe something they call a phai-trap — a circle of garden hose covered with nylon nooses set around a tethered pigeon. The hawk walks across the nooses to get to the bait.

When I was in the Rocky Mountain area, I used the conventional bow net with some success. It has been successfully used in Europe and the Near East for centuries. Too bulky to carry in a car, it is far better suited for a pickup truck. We constructed ours with the bases of the curved limb of the bow fastened by wire to two of the largest rat traps we could get. When the bow is pulled back and held by a long monofilament line fastened to a blind some distance away, it is quite effective. The tethered pigeon is placed in the center, and when the hawk strikes the bait, the bow is released by cutting or snipping the line that holds back the bow net. The mesh should be the same color and size as that for the dho-gazza trap.

It's possible to get involved in the details of trapping systems used in Holland and in the British Isles since bygone days. But remember that all these methods boil down to a fairly simple matter of common sense. The basic bow nets and dho-gazza nets were the backbone of trapping gear.

Hal Webster and Frank Beebe, two of the country's most experienced falconers, have come up with what I consider a great development in trapping large falcons and accipiters. I don't know if they originated it, but I have never run across it in any other falconry literature.

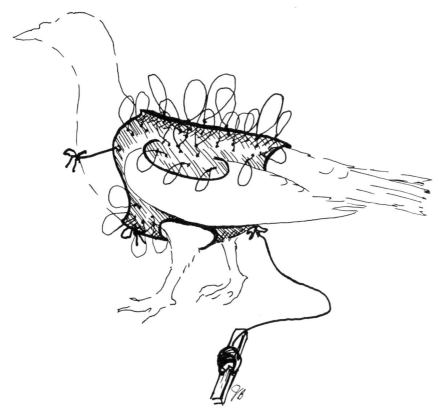

Pigeon wearing harness to which line is attached.

It is a simple leather harness that fits over the back, sides, and underside of a common barnyard pigeon, and has holes through which the pigeon's feet and wings can protrude. The pigeon can both walk and fly when the harness is attached. This rig is covered with from 50 to 75 nylon nooses of varying strength. Twelve-pound mono should be enough for prairie falcons and Cooper's hawks, but I think 15-pound mono should be used for anything bigger. A smaller harness can be made for a starling-sized bird, and I am sure it would take sharp-shinned and pigeon hawks.

The nooses are fastened to the leather harness. Webster's secret to keep them from pulling out is to pass them through a tiny glass bead on the inside of the leather. These small beads are about the size used in making Indian-type moccasins. The harness is fastened in the front, and a nylon line of about 15 to 20 feet is attached to the harness as shown. A short link of rubber or other elastic material is attached between the line and the harness. This link absorbs the shock in case the hawk tries to fly off with the pigeon and harness and gets yanked by the trailing line. A small wooden peg can be tied to the far end of the line with the line wound around it. This arrangement keeps the line from becoming tangled and also tends to slow down a hawk trying to make off with the bird and harness.

It is a handy method of trapping falcons and big accipiters, and the technique for using it is simple. A pigeon is held loosely in the hand while the falconer is cruising in a car or four-wheel-drive vehicle across country or along a beach. When a hunting hawk is spotted, the pigeon is tossed into the air. It tries to fly off but doesn't get far because of the weight of the harness and the line. But the pigeon does get far enough to attract the hawk, which may strike it immediately or light near it to observe its movements for a while. As when you use the wire-net trap with nooses, the vehicle should continue until the hawk has fastened to its prey and becomes entangled. If the hawk is big enough, it may try to fly off with the pigeon and line. But even a big gyrfalcon or goshawk cannot keep it up for long. Either the weight brings it to the ground or the line fouls in a tree or bush.

This system does away with all heavy gear and provides you with great mobility.

7

Your New Hawk— The Sparrow Hawk

SO HERE YOU are, novice falconer, with a new hawk. What now?

Whether the hawk is a falcon or an accipiter, whether an eyas (young from the nest), passager (immature hawk on its first migration), or a haggard (adult several or more years old), you'll have the same basic problem at first: to calm down the hawk and get it accustomed to its new owner and its new environment. Obviously, a hawk fresh from a nest will be less frightened of a human being than an adult bird would be. It is easy to see why the old and experienced haggard hawk —fresh trapped—would be most skittish of all. Nevertheless, the treatment of both the passager and haggard hawks should be the same.

Leather jesses (illustrated and explained in the chapter on equipment) should be fastened to the legs as soon as possible after capture. A leash or length of leather should be fastened to the jesses and the other end of the leash should be fastened to a perch in a dark room. Darkness keeps diurnal birds from flying. They roost or perch and sleep at night. Since they are prey to such nocturnal predators as larger owls and tree-climbing carnivores (bobcats, martins, fishers, weasels, and such), they perch quiet and still in the dark. Therefore the hawk is kept in a darkened room until it has calmed down and become accustomed to the idea that it is not being attacked or hurt. This is also the theory behind the use of the leather hood. The hood simply simulates darkness when the hawk is being transported in the daytime.

The type of perch you should use for the new hawk depends upon its species. The bigger falcons, which spend much of their lives resting and nesting on rocky ledges, find a hard block perch most comfortable. Since the accipiters and several of the smaller falcons (the pigeon hawk and the sparrow hawk) prefer roosting and resting on tree branches, they are better adapted to the ring, bow, and T perches. However, the first perch a newly acquired hawk should be placed upon is a screen perch. The bird should be tied by the end of the leash with a falconer's knot to the padded crossbar of this perch. This perch is used only until the hawk gets out of the habit of "bating," another Old World term for just flying wildly off the perch or wrist because of rage or fear. All these items are described and illustrated in detail in the chapter on equipment.

A curtain of canvas is hung down from the perching bar and weighted at the bottom. Canvas has been traditionally considered the best material because a hawk cannot become enmeshed in its weave and hang upside down. But a heavy polyurethane sheet might do as well today. When the hawk flies from the bar, it will simply swing below it and hang against the canvas. When it finds itself upside down, it will scramble back up on top of the perch. If the canvas were not there, the hawk might climb back up all right each time it flew off and dangled. But if it flew up enough times on the same side of the perch, its leash would get increasingly shorter until it might run out of leash. Finally it would fall off and die hanging by feet lashed to the perch. The exact height of this perch is not important, but since a hawk gets nervous when a human stands above it, shoulder height at least would be wise.

The first few weeks of captivity are most important. Falconers in olden days slept beside the cages, keeping a candle or a lantern lit most of the time and stroking and quietly talking to the birds. A gentle voice, slow movement, and constant encouragement from the falconer are vital in these early stages if the hawk is to accept and tolerate its new partner. I have raised and flown many hawks. I believe there can be a degree of communication between a human being and a hawk, but never that relationship of love and trust we enjoy with such animals as dogs, horses, and a few other pets. A hawk may come to rely upon you for food, exercise, and hunting experience, but a tacit acceptance is the most you can expect from your hawk.

I have been fascinated by the birds of prey all my life. I admire them for their fierceness, their clean-lined beauty, their dazzling speed,

This tiny sparrow hawk is just out of the nest.

their courage, and their reckless abandon on the wing. They are independence personified. Since the beginning of time, men have admired hawks for the same reasons I admire them. I do not ask for the love of a falcon. I ask only to be allowed to share in some part its single-mindedness. It is uncomplicated, classic — the ultimate in efficient design. When I want love from an animal, I raise Labrador retrievers and German short-haired pointers.

The newly acquired hawk must be induced to take food. It may not do this for several days, but hawks are independent, not stupid. When they get hungry, and they do each day, they will react to freshly killed meat. I have often imagined they take food so soon after capture because of some instinct that tells them to keep up their strength so that escape might be easier. At any rate, even the most traumatically trapped hawk will eventually succumb to the temptation of fresh meat. That is the beginning of acceptance of man, although each hawk has its own timetable in arriving at this compromise.

At this stage of breaking a hawk to the presence of a human, it is most important to make sure the door to the darkened room always stays closed — to prevent any predators such as dogs or cats from getting at the helpless bird, and to make sure the hawk is not perched in a damp area with a cold draft blowing on it. Hawks, like most other living creatures, can catch cold. They seldom perch in damp, drafty places in the wild, even though they might be caught in a downpour.

I cannot tell you how long it will take for a captured hawk to gentle down and stop frantically resisting attempts to approach it slowly or hold it on a gloved fist. It takes a lot of time — that I can say with certainty. I have gentled some hawks in days and have spent months with others. Also, there is no hard-and-fast formula for the number of hours a day or night you must spend with a hawk to "man" the bird, or gentle it. The time in the "mew" — the darkened room to which a falconer brings a new hawk — varies with the wildness of each bird and with the degree of trauma experienced in its capture. Incidentally, the word "mew" comes from an Old World term for molting — the shedding of certain feathers each year, which then grow back.

I have seen Jim, my son, gentle a wild-caught adult sparrow hawk in several days. Some people just have a way with wild things; Jim is such a person. I saw him gentle a passager red-tailed hawk in a matter of weeks until it was almost as tame as a dog. But only with him. In just several weeks, I also have gentled wild-trapped adult hawks to the point where they would fly from 20 yards away to my fist for food. I have also spent months on hawks that were given to me and eventually had to give up on them because they were untamable and unmanageable.

The last time I visited Hal Webster at his home near Denver, he had in a mew a prairie falcon which he admitted would never respond to any sort of gentling. He'd had it some time. Each time he opened the door to its room, it would bate — smash itself against walls and hurl itself into corners in a frenzy. Like humans, there are hawks with defects, and a falconer can do little with them. I suppose they are not much different from bird dogs in that respect. I have seen pure-bred bird dogs that would not hunt; they had no interest in game, had no "nose," and there was no apparent reason for their inability to find birds. I know one magnificent 85-pound pure-bred male Labrador retriever that not only cannot swim but hates the water. I also knew of a pretty little English setter female that belonged to my close friend and humor editor of *Field & Stream*, Ed Zern, that literally could not find Ed in his own living room if he did not move so she could see him. She had no sense of smell at all. Ed loved the dog, a gentle housedog and a good watchdog, but he would rather not discuss her hunting qualities.

But back to the gentling of hunting hawks. This process is simply aimed to set up some form of communication between human and bird.

There's no formula for how long it will take to gentle a hawk such as this female sparrow hawk.

Until the hawk stops fearing the falconer, no training to hunt can begin. It is a long time from the moment of capture — when the hawk, screaming in rage and defiance, falls on its back with wings spread, beak open, and talons straining to sink into a hand — to when that same hawk will perch on a gloved hand within inches of your face, accept food from your hand, and allow you to stroke gently its breast feathers.

The gap between these two extremes is shortened only by the long hours in a semidarkened room, the falconer gently stroking and talking to the hawk. During this time, the constant sound of a voice is all important. The old-time falconers found that blowing a little smoke from a pipe toward the hawk now and then taught it to accept the presence of man sooner. I suppose the bird began to associate the smell of tobacco with the calm voice and the absence of fear and anger.

A soft Indian-style hood can be placed on the hawk's head at this stage if you intend to break the bird to the hood. Experts now differ on the need of a hawk to be hooded because the means of transporting hawks have changed. The original need for hoods, they say, was to keep a hawk from flying off the wrist when a man was walking in the field or riding a horse. They say that hawks now can be transported in cars, which run smoother. The hawks can ride on a car perch, a simple perch rigged to clamp on the back of a car seat.

I have found, however, that hawks will fly from the wrist for many reasons besides motion. They will take to the air if startled by any number of things — dogs, people, and sudden loud noises and changes of light. I have found it far easier to carry a hawk accustomed to a hood than one that is not. This is especially true in areas where there are many people. A hawk that is very calm if gentled and trained on a farm or a ranch may be startled frequently by people, animals, and the various machinery and gadgets found in today's busy suburb.

Your hawk by now should have had a pair of jesses put on it so it could be tied to its perch. Putting on jesses is a simple task if you have handled hawks before. If you have not, it can be a battle royal. It is advisable to have two people put jesses on a newly caught hawk — one to hold the hawk gently from the rear, pinning its wings to its sides and holding its legs well above where the jesses are to be fastened. If the hawk happens to be a big one, even this procedure can be chaotic. I have seen large red-tailed hawks break loose from the person holding them. And sometimes, even if the person keeps a grip on the legs, the hawk can deliver severe blows with its huge wings. Strangely enough, hawks do not often bite when angry or frightened. They rely mostly upon their talons for defense. Nevertheless, I have been nipped painfully several times, by a Cooper's hawk and by a golden eagle.

If you want to use the technique of slipping a part of a woman's nylon stocking over a hawk to keep it calm while changing jesses, it is best to do this while the hawk is either hooded or in almost complete darkness. It will fight less if it cannot see. The stocking section is slid down over the tail feathers when the jesses are tied. Either the traditional jesses or the Aylmeri jesses can be used.

The Aylmeri jesses are preferred over the traditional jesses by many falconers, who say they are less likely to catch in brush, branches, or wire fences, and thus leave a bird hanging or break its legs. I suppose this is true, but I prefer the traditional jesses for nostalgic reasons; and with the introduction of the ball swivel between the sections of the old jesses, there is much less chance for a bird to twist them around its feet. How to put on jesses can be figured out easily by looking at the illustrations of the jesses. During the "manning" of the new hawk, and while performing such tasks as putting on jesses and hoods, leather welder's gloves should be worn if the hawk is any larger than the tiny sparrow hawk. A pair of ordinary leather gloves will be enough for the small bird. However, even the relatively small sharp-shinned hawk can sink needle-sharp talons through a light glove.

Anyone who has never been grabbed by a large hawk, such as a goshawk or falcon, has quite an experience coming! Not only is it extremely painful, but the danger of infection is great. A hawk's feet, used to rip up meat, are contaminated by particles clinging to the talons. Also, when a hawk kills for food, it is accustomed to having the victim struggle in its claws. The natural reaction of a hawk is to squeeze repeatedly until the struggles cease. That's when the hawk can assume its prey is dead and ready to be eaten. Man's instinctive reaction to being grabbed is to try to force the hawk to release its grip. Unfortunately, this usually causes the hawk to clamp down harder. The strength of a large hawk's grip is amazing. Multiply that several times and you can imagine how an eagle's grip feels, even through a welder's glove.

The hawk is fastened to its screen perch by a length of leather leash secured to the jesses, with the end of the leash tied to the perch by a falconer's knot. I prefer this version of the knot — used by Hal Webster

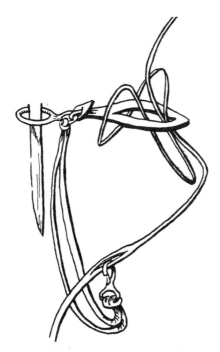

This version of the falconer's knot has safeguards and shortcuts that are missing in the traditional falconer's knot.

and several others — because it has some shortcuts and safeguards that are lacking in the traditional falconer's knot. The falconer's knot is a simple, yet strong, knot that must be tied with one hand because the other hand is busy holding a hawk. The modified knot illustrated here provides the safety of the heavy rubber band to cushion shock should a bird leave the perch and reach the end of the leash. This knot also utilizes a separate leather ring, which removes a step from the tying process.

With your new hawk installed in the mew, all you must do now, for an indeterminable length of time, is to spend as much time as possible with the bird each day until it stops fearing you and taking off from the perch each time you approach. Only the falconer should feed the bird, and it is best if not too many other people come close to it until it gentles down.

Don't worry about giving the hawk water. A hawk requires very little drinking water, getting most of its required fluid from the meat it eats. Some hawks, however, like to bathe, and later a pan can be kept near its perch. The hawk should eat all of its meals from the hand of the falconer at this stage. It must come to associate food with the human and not simply be left food to eat while alone. Chunks of raw beef can be too bulky for a hawk, which is liable to bolt food at this point in its training. Beef, cut into strips, is far preferable. Try to get the hawk to eat voluntarily. Force-feeding a hawk by cramming food down its throat while another person holds it may provide the needed food and keep the hawk alive, but it does nothing to establish a compatible relationship between bird and owner. Try drawing the strips of meat slowly across the hawk's toes. It will now and then eat by instinct.

What I have said so far has been somewhat general. I should add a number of specific things about gentling a hunting hawk. Since most beginning falconers today must pass the falconer examinations for a trapping permit, let us assume you acquire the tiny sparrow hawk. (It is possible to get a gyrfalcon or a peregrine falcon by permit and by trapping, but the possession of such a bird by a novice falconer is highly unlikely.) It is important to remember that falcons, regardless of size, are falcons. The intelligent and easily trained sparrow hawk or North American kestrel (*Falco sparverius*) has the same qualities as its slightly larger cousin the pigeon hawk, or European merlin. The European merlin (*Falco columbarius aesalon*) is generally the same bird as our pigeon hawk of the east coast (*Falco columbarius columbarius*), but there are two subspecies in North America. The western pigeon hawk is called (*Falco columbarius benderi*), and there is another in the northern-central plains (*Falco columbarius richardsoni*) or Richardson's Merlin.

These three subspecies of the pigeon hawk, and the sparrow hawk, are trained very much the same way as would be the larger falcons. So for the sake of brevity, while I'm talking about training the little sparrow hawk, we can assume that the same methods would work on all falcons. There might be a few differences, however, that would be worth mentioning in the beginning.

The sparrow hawk has a tendency to be a "screamer" . . . more than other falcons. So when you're taking one from the nest of an eyas, the young bird should not be taken until it is just about ready to fly.

When I first began collecting hawks, I would take young sparrow hawks when they were but tiny balls of white down. They invariably developed into screamers, and unfortunately had to be released to the wild. The trait comes from the young birds' habit in the nest of setting up a high-pitched chattering call when they catch sight of a parent bird approaching with food.

When these birds are taken from the nest too early, they tend to "imprint" upon humans. So when they're approached with (or without) food, they set up a clamor that can become unnerving. To prevent this with the little falcons, try to wait until they are 28 to 30 days old. By then they will be almost ready to fly and will have shed the down except for a few small spots on the head. It is usually a good idea to remove the young of any falcon from a nest toward evening. At that time of day the young should have fed and will have a full crop, making the long trip to your home easier.

Something also should be said about the method of transporting young hawks just out of the nest, in vehicles and by hand. I once injured a young red-tailed hawk, coming down a tree with it stuffed inside my shirtfront. I was young and didn't realize the young hawk could be hurt by getting caught between my chest and the tree trunk. The best way to prevent them from injury while you take them from a tree or a ledge nest is to place them in a cloth or burlap sack and lower them by rope to a friend on the ground.

After getting them to a car, the best way to transport them home is to place them in a cardboard box with gunny sacking in the bottom. The sack — stretched tightly across the bottom of the box — enables the baby hawks to cling to something firm with their talons while being transported.

The best place to keep very young hawks just brought home to the loft is in an artificial nest — a cardboard or wooden box lined with wood shavings. In the case of sparrow hawks, a good idea is to build an artificial tree with some dead branches and place it so that as the young birds grow, they can fly from one branch to another.

When you first begin to feed meat to your young hawk, offer the meat on the end of a stick or by using forceps — rather than the fingers. This approach will prevent the hawk from being frightened by the size of the human hand at first. I have found with sparrow hawks that they thrive much better on mice and sparrows than they do on strips of lean beef — although such lean beef strips will do until the better food comes along. It is best if the young hawks are fed three times a day at first. Later, twice a day.

It is necessary to give them the fur of mice and feather of sparrows only once a week to serve as a casting. This bulk — which they will regurgitate as a fur and feather pellet — serves to keep them healthy.

Make sure both the mice and sparrows (which you can easily trap) are fresh-killed when offered to hawks as food. The birds should be plucked and the mice skinned most of the time when used as food. Don't worry about leaving the internals inside when feeding the hawks. The intestines are good for them.

When first beginning to feed the young hawks, make sure the meat is tied down — one way or another. Some falconers like to feed hawks on boards. I prefer to start them out on the gloved fist. I don't see much point in having to train them later to leave the board for the fist. The meat can be gripped between the thumb and forefinger of the glove to keep the hawk from picking it up easily. This routine is so that the hawk cannot drag the meat about and learn any bad habits early.

If a new or young hawk will not begin to eat when it is being "manned" or gentled in a partially lit room, try this: Place the meat on the hawk's feet, and then either move your fingers inside the glove or reach over and pinch the bird's toes. That contact will cause it to look down, and it will find the meat. It is easy for you to gradually make the hawk step from the edge of the screen perch or block to your gloved hand by slowly moving your hand away with meat on it. Each day the hawk will take a longer step, then a longer jump. In time, the bird will be eating the meat at the same level as the eyes of the falconer — when it should have gotten over the fear of that particular human — at least in the partly darkened room where it is being fed. It is only a short step from there to feeding it out in the open, but there — at least for a time — it will likely "bate" (fly wildly) from the wrist at all sorts of strange sights and sounds.

It should now be a simple matter to take your hawk from its perch in the mew to the outdoors. Always move slowly with hawks. They are jumpy and nervous by nature, and the slightest quick or jerky movement will send them off a perch or a gloved hand. To get the hawk to step from a perch or block, place your gloved hand *behind* the legs, not in front, and raise slowly up against the back of the legs.

Be careful that there are no dogs or cats — or, for that matter, strange people — about when you take the hawk outside for its training periods. These periods, incidentally, should always be at feeding time. Hawks are more alert then and easier to make behave. A hawk is most nervous when something is either behind or above it. It is always best to kneel or sit down beside a new hawk. If possible, don't let people walk behind a hawk while it is being manned or trained. Hawks tend to crane their necks about and attempt to leave the perch.

For best results in training a hawk, the bird's weight should be considered. Weight can be an intangible sort of thing sometimes, but several factors should be taken into account. A bird should have an ideal weight — one that is just right for his or her body after exercise, or before. Certain factors affect bird weight: the type of food being fed, the age of the bird, its species, the weather, the season, and how long the bird has been in captivity. A postage scale can be rigged up to a bench and a perch fitted to the top of it so that a hawk can be weighed while perching. It is important that your scale be accurate. It should be graduated in ¼-ounce increments for the smaller hawks and in ½-ounce for the larger. The hawk should be weighed at the same time each day, and with the same equipment on: hoods, jesses, bells, whatever.

For the novice with a small sparrow hawk, such a bird should weigh from 7½ to 8½ ounces — depending upon whether it is a male or female. It would be foolish to start out with a male sparrow hawk if you intend to hunt it. The beautiful little bird will tame easily and train just as well, but the larger and more aggressive female makes a far better hunter. In taking the very young from a nest, it is difficult to tell the sexes apart. But wild-trapped sparrow hawks are easy to come by. My son and I trapped several a day for banding, and I know falconers who have trapped 30 or 40 in one day during the fall migration.

When your sparrow hawk has been in training a few weeks and is handling well, it can be put out on blocks in the weathering ground. It is usually a good idea to put the new hawk out the first time in the evening. Hawks are more docile and quiet at this time of day. Each day, put the hawk out a little earlier until it grows accustomed to the grounds and the block.

But be careful of hot, direct sunlight. It's a good idea to put a block where the hawk can fly into the shade when the sun gets too hot. Put out a shallow container of water for its bath in the middle of the day. A hawk will sometimes take a bath if it has sunlight in which to dry itself.

8

Flying to Fist and Lure
—Kestrel/Sparrow Hawk

THE STAGE BETWEEN gentling your hawk in a darkened room and hunting with it in the field for live birds or small game is very important. A mistake during this period can spoil a hawk for the future. And remember, your hawk is to be fed only on the gloved fist during the familiarization period. It is never left to eat alone on a perch or on the floor or ground.

The hawk is now taken outside on the gloved fist and, with the leash and jesses securely fastened to the glove, it can be walked about. This will not cause any undue excitement for a young bird. Hawks are naturally curious. A young one will bob its head and stare at things new to it. However, if your bird is a wild-trapped hawk, for a while it is likely to bate, that is fly wildly from the fist at the sight of people, dogs, vehicles, and anything new. Since the leash is shortened to only about a foot, it is easy to put the hawk back on the fist.

I prefer to carry a hawk several days with the hood on, getting it accustomed to the motion of riding on a fist without becoming frightened. The hood can be taken off several days later and the hawk taught that there is nothing to fear as long as it is riding on the falconer's glove.

An example of a Dutch hood.

The time necessary for the hawk to learn this, obviously, will vary with the distractions of the surroundings and the nature and experience of the bird.

At this stage, a hawk should be fed three times a day, but only a small amount of beef strips at a time. This routine gives the falconer a chance to try to make the bird hop or fly to the gloved fist more than once a day. As a matter of fact, it can be made to fly to the fist as many times as you want it to. But the first few times it is best to settle for a few hops and/or a short flight before gently putting the hawk back on its perch.

The technique is quite simple: With the hawk on the perch, crouch down the first time a few yards away, with a few small strips of beef resting on the glove. Call the hawk to you. Any sound you choose is all right so long as the call remains consistent throughout the training. Some falconers call the hawk's name repeatedly, some whistle a note of their own choosing, and some use an instrument, such as a police or dog whistle. I tried to imitate the natural call of the hawk. A sparrow hawk is not difficult to imitate, nor is the call of most buteos, or soaring hawks. The call of a peregrine, gyrfalcon, and prairie falcon is a sort of rapid staccato *cac-cac-cac-cac-cac*. I have the most difficulty imitating the call of accipiters, and usually just call the name or whistle.

If the falconer is lucky on the first try, the hawk will instantly fly from its perch to the glove or from the perch to the ground and then to the glove. Whichever of these it does, the move should be regarded as a triumph. Many hawks will simply remain on the perch, refusing to fly to the gloved hand for days, sometimes weeks. Eventually, because of hunger, all will usually come around. Once they do, the falconer is on his or her way toward training the bird to hunt.

In succeeding days, the falconer can extend the distance of the daily flights by fastening a long, stout cord to the leash and tying it securely to the perch. It is still a thrill for me today to watch a hawk fly some distance to the wrist, particularly to the wrist of a young falconer. The instant of landing is a spectacular thing to watch, establishing between the falconer and a hawk a strange bond difficult to explain to someone who has never experienced it. It can be topped only by the feeling a falconer gets when he sees his or her hawk fly to the fist the first time it is flown free. At that moment, the falconer knows all the training has not been in vain.

After the hawk has gotten the idea that flying to the wrist for food is the accepted pattern, it seems to become sort of fun for the hawk — if a hawk can be said to have fun. I think they can, and I also think certain hawks have mean streaks and others a sort of sense of humor. If you think not, you have not seen many hawks in the wild, where they will sometimes dive upon and harass other birds just for something to do. They are obviously not hungry and, after tiring of the sport, will allow the harried game to escape while they soar off into the distance or rest for a bit in some tree. Flight games with their mates, young, and other hawks certainly seem to be played for sheer enjoyment.

It is now time for training to the lure, one of the most vital steps in the process of teaching a hawk not only to take its food daily from the lure but also to stay with it until the falconer gently reaches down and picks up the hawk on his gloved fist. I will be talking primarily about the falcons when I discuss the lure. It is not nearly so necessary to use one regularly on a short-winged hawk. They are ultrasimplistic in their attitude toward the kill. Teaching one to fly to a lure and to eat from it is fine, because it simulates the quarry you want the hawk to chase in the field; but only a falcon will dive, climb, and pursue a swinging lure. The accipiters will for a while, but they tend to become bored. A sharp-shinned, Cooper's or goshawk is far better trained just to go after any bird or small game released.

The quarry at the training stage can be anything from white mice and hamsters to wild pigeons and wild-trapped rabbits. Naturally the smarter and faster an accipiter hawk gets, the more sophisticated game it can be flown at. If the accipiter has been well trained to fly to the gloved fist for food, it should be possible, for example, for the falconer to approach the hawk slowly after it has killed a pheasant or a rabbit and, with some meat showing clearly on the glove, insert the glove and meat between the hawk and the newly killed game. The hawk should reach out for the food and step on the glove at the same time.

A dangerous step must be taken just before teaching a falcon to fly to the lure; it must be allowed to fly free. This is when many hawks are lost either because the training was not sufficient or because the hawk has a strong desire for freedom causing it to fly away as soon as it thinks it is free. The modern light monofilament fishing lines, however, have made such loss less likely. On all the flights the hawk has been coming to the fist up to this time — including flights of up to several hundred yards — it has been held by a light line. However, this line is so light that it is doubtful if the hawk realizes it is carrying it. Yet when it does make its first flight, it is doubtful if it will realize it is *not* still fastened to the line.

So the first free flight of a hawk should not be faced with dread at all. It should be prepared for, however, with serious thought. Make sure the flight is made in an area where the hawk will not be distracted by other people, dogs, or vehicles. It should also be hungry, so do not feed it that day before the first flight. Simply place the hawk gently on its accustomed perch and let it get accustomed to sitting there a while. Then approach slowly and unsnap the leash from the jesses. Walk slowly away until you have reached the distance you want the hawk to fly, and then turn around. With fresh meat on the glove, point the fist slightly above eye level and call the hawk. It should — as usual — fly directly to your wrist. Try not to consider it any different from all previous flights, although when it is over a little celebration of the event would be appropriate!

I remember flying my first hawk free for the first time, just as clearly as I remember my first solo flight as a student pilot. I can remember saying to myself before each event: "Now this is not going to be any different from all the other times — relax." The heck it wasn't!

After that first successful flight in a quiet place in familiar surroundings, the next step after carrying the falcon for several days on the wrist in the wilds should be to let it soar up to a nearby tree in an area where there are no distractions. This should also be done with the accipiter hawks. Allow the hawk to remain in the tree for a few moments while you walk away, then turn with meat on the glove and repeat the performance you did a few days before. The hawk should do exactly the same as it did before. When that happens, you can be relatively sure you have a hawk that will return to you when you want it to.

Remember the lure. Take another look at the illustration in the chapter on equipment. It has a swivel at the head and laces to which fresh meat is tied. The lure should be fastened to the end of a stout cord 12 to 15 feet long.

In a wide-open space (again, with no distraction), place the bird on its perch. It is not necessary that it be allowed to fly free here. There is no need to unsnap the leash from the jesses. When it has settled comfortably, walk away thirty to forty feet, wearing the falconer's bag in which the lure is always carried. Take the lure out with your back to the hawk, make sure fresh meat is fastened to it, and unroll the cord from it. Turn around and face the hawk and toss the lure several yards in front of you. The hawk may or may not fly to it immediately, because it has been trained to fly to the gloved fist for food and it sees no gloved fist. Twitch the lure a few times to get the attention of the bird. If the hawk refuses to fly to it at all, pick the lure up and move closer until the bird flies. However, the first time a falcon flies to the lure, call it a day. Don't try again until the following day. From the wrist to the lure is quite a transition for a hawk.

After the hawk has become accustomed to flying directly to the lure on the ground, it should be taught to fly to the lure while the lure is being swung about the falconer in circles. It is necessary for the hawk to be free during this exercise. Otherwise the bird would become entangled with the falconer if it were flying about him while tied to the light line. However, by this time the falconer should be reasonably sure his hawk won't try to escape.

What we are trying to do here is simple: The hawk must be exercised frequently to stay in good shape. Flying to the lure is the only way a hawk can be exercised outside of actually hunting it in the field, and that obviously cannot be done all year. If the bird is young, it is also being taught to catch its food in mid-air. I have always considered flying a falcon to the lure almost as much fun as hunting one—especially if it is a strong, wild-caught bird. A falcon can easily catch the lure no matter how difficult the falconer tries to make the swing.

Ever since falconry began, there have been all sorts of recommendations as to how a lure should be swung to exercise a hawk. It is mostly common sense and individual preference, depending on the age, experience, and strength of the falcon. Slow, gentle, and relatively flat swings are sometimes plenty for a young eyas, while a tough old wild-caught haggard can catch the lure anywhere you want to swing it. Many hawks enjoy flying to a lure each day. It is a great sight to watch.

It is important to remember that the lure should be swung only as long as the hawk needs the exercise. As soon as it shows any signs of tiredness or boredom, the lure should be allowed to drop to the ground, where the hawk may feed on it.

A really strong falcon will make spectacular dives or stoops at a swinging lure 20 or 30 times before tiring. The only risk in flying constantly to the lure is that both the falconer and the falcon will come to regard this as the ultimate fun and the falcon will become "lure bound" as the Old World saying goes. All this flying, however, in addition to keeping the hawk in good shape, is to keep it ready to hunt. Hunting a hawk is the ultimate thrill of falconry, but flying a falcon to a lure is far better than not flying it at anything.

Hawks on the lure — feeding, that is — are easily spooked by someone approaching. For that reason, always approach carefully a feeding hawk on the lure. Don't tower over it. Try to stoop or sidle up to it slowly. If it stops feeding and looks at you, stop until it has settled down again.

Launching itself from block perch, peregrine falcon flies to meat on falconer's glove.

Don't stare at a hawk. It makes them nervous. I suppose it is because, like most wild creatures, they don't like a fixed stare. Maybe it is a prelude to being charged by a predator.

The trouble with frightening a hawk off a lure is that such action sows the seeds of "carrying." A hawk that tries to fly off a lure — attempting to take the meat with it — will in time try to carry off the game it has killed. This is one of the most troublesome habits of some hawks and can be a source of frustration to a falconer.

I once had a female goshawk who developed the nasty habit of completely shielding any meat she had from me. She would crouch over it — wings and tail feathers forming an umbrella — and glare at me or anyone else who tried to come close. We tried for months to get her to calm down while feeding, but never succeeded. She would hunt well — being a fierce old girl that had been wild-trapped. But when she killed, she tried to make off with the game each time. Finally she flew away one day with a small cottontail she had killed at the edge of an open field. We never found her.

With a new hawk, particularly a young one that has been taken from the nest, it is always smart to offer bits of meat scraps from the gloved fingers to a hawk feeding upon a lure. This routine makes the hawk more relaxed and accustomed to eating on the ground. Such experience is especially important if a new hawk has been eating only on the fist. To make the hawk stay with the lure while eating, either use a heavy lure or fasten the light flying lure to the ground in some manner.

It's important to fly a hawk to the lure in areas where the bird will not get hung up. A back yard with a lawn is a good spot. Since the hawk, particularly a sparrow hawk, can easily be discouraged if the creance (long line) becomes entangled while flying at a lure, I use a six-pound-test monofilament line in flying such small hawks. I suppose I could use four-pound, but I must admit to a certain amount of uncertainty about that line's holding when a bird gets hung up. Even the slightest twig or weed stem can bring down a sparrow hawk while flying on such a line, so be sure the area is free of obstacles.

Teaching your small hawk to stoop to a lure can be fun, but there are some rules you must follow. First, use a light lure — about 1½ ounces. With meat fastened to the light lure and the hawk on a perch or on the fist of an assistant, start the lure and toss it to the turf close to the hawk. When the bird flies to it, twitch it away just before the bird lands on it. This action will probably confuse the bird. It will either hop about on the ground looking for the lure or will circle above.

Whichever the bird does, throw the lure back close to it and allow the hawk to feed from the meat. The teaching process is just a matter of making it more and more difficult for the bird to seize the lure each time. Finally, if the hawk is eager and strong, it will be chasing the lure back and forth on the ground and attempting to catch it in mid-air. This is the objective — training a hawk to catch game in mid-air.

Don't worry if your small sparrow hawk — after trying to catch the lure in the air, falls to the ground with its beak open and panting. The bird is not in condition for this violent exercise, and it won't be so for some time.

The beautiful little sparrow hawks are by nature great hoverers. They can be seen in every state in the Union, hovering in mid-air as they stare down at their prey. The falconer can use this natural trait to get a sparrow hawk to "wait on" or stay overhead until game is flushed.

Best way to begin is to wait for a day with a brisk wind. Then take the tiny hawk out and have a friend hold it on fist some distance away from you. When you reach into the bag where the lure is always kept and bring the lure forth, with meat fastened to it, the hawk should take off and fly toward you.

When it reaches you, conceal the lure — either by hand or by dropping it into grass at your feet. If the grass is tall enough the hawk probably won't land in it. Instead it will face into the wind and hover over you — looking for the lure. If you don't produce the lure and simply walk upwind, the hawk should circle you as you do. Don't keep the hawk up there too long. It may become discouraged. After a moment or so, produce the lure and throw it for the hawk.

This practice can be repeated each day until the hawk stays overhead in the wind — waiting above the falconer for the lure to appear. It's a good idea to occasionally bring the lure up through the glove and call the hawk down to the fist to keep it accustomed to returning to the glove when called.

The wind helps in such training to hover, but don't take a young hawk out in days of high winds. If your hawk has any tendency to stray, a high wind makes it easier. A hawk can be swept away and lost.

Also, be sure to stop the training as the light begins to fail late in the day. You'll find it tough enough to train a hawk in good light. Some birds are loathe to return to the fist or to a hood when they cannot see well.

All this training is dependent upon the hawk's condition. If its weight is holding up well and the hawk is enthusiastic, keep up the training. If weight or enthusiasm falls off, let the bird rest a few days.

9

To Hack or
Not to Hack?

BECAUSE THIS IS a falconry primer and not a detailed manual of the sport, I will not spend a great deal of space on hacking new hawks. However, I do think it is good for the beginning falconer to know what hacking is and how to do it.

In America today, the human population density is so great in most areas that the average city dweller or even the suburban novice falconer just will not have the room to hack eyasses — young hawks recently taken from the nest. And again, with hawks so valuable today, not many falconers want to risk losing young hawks at hack.

Hacking young hawks is the practice of letting hawks fend for themselves in a localized area until they are able to kill for themselves. Then they are "taken up" and confined.

Advocates of hacking say this practice not only teaches hawks to hunt and kill on their own but also rapidly strengthens muscles and develops flying power in the weeks spent in freedom. All that is probably true. It is hardly possible for the part-time falconer, swinging a lure, to develop his young hawk as rapidly or as well. But in this age of high population and rapid development of suburbs, we have to make compromises.

However, for the falconer who lives on a farm or ranch and has plenty of space to raise and train hawks, hacking is a time-proven method of raising strong, fast hunting hawks. There are as many systems of hack as there are books about falconry — and there have been books written about this sport for centuries.

This, basically, is what hack is: When taken from the eyrie or nest — at about the point where they are able to fly — young hawks are brought home. Then, instead of being placed in a loft or mew to start their exposure to man, they are equipped with jesses (without the slit at the end where the creance is fastened, to prevent the young hawks from getting hung up on a branch or wire) and bells. Bells can be omitted if the hawk is as tiny as a sparrow hawk, as the weight will handicap the tiny hawk in chasing prey. Then the hawks are placed in a large box — outside. By outside I mean in the center of a large yard or field with some trees close by so that the hawks may fly up and perch for observation.

Box size will vary with the falconer, but let's say the box is a 6'x 6' square. It is also 6' high — with a roof. It can be open on one side — preferably that side facing away from prevailing winds. The young birds — say, two eyasses — are placed inside on a floor covered with wood shavings. A board about a foot wide and a yard long is placed inside the house with meat tied to it for each hawk. The food is tied down so the hawks cannot drag it away or fly off with it. The birds are left overnight in the "hack house."

By the following day, the hawks will have learned to climb to the top of the box or house. They should be fed the same way each day — three times a day, but the board should be placed on top of the house. The food — depending upon what type of hawks are being raised — should be close to what they will be eating in the wild. This means sparrows, mice, small rabbits, or starlings. The meat should be cut up and tied down to the board.

By this time — say a week or so — the young hawks should be losing the last of their down and should be flying fairly well. They should be perching in the trees close to the house by now and flying down to the top of it to eat. When the flight feathers have grown hard and are no longer filled with blood, the young are said to be "hard-penned" and are ready to fly for game. When the young hawks are flying each day for their own food, the meals provided by the falconer can be reduced to two a day. All the previous meat should be cleaned up each time before new meat is served, and the board should be kept clean at all times.

Bow net can be set on top of the hack house and baited with fresh meat.

In about three or four weeks, one or two of the hawks should have stopped coming to the board for every meal. It may be skipping one meal a day because it is able to catch wild game. Most veteran falconers agree this is the time to catch them up — both birds — and return them to a loft of blocks to continue their training.

This form of hacking is valuable from another viewpoint. It enables the falconer to study the birds as they fly after game. That way it is relatively easy to gain some idea of their hunting and flying style and their potential. It is also a matter of record that hacked hawks are less liable to be screamers.

Catching up these young hawks that can fly is not as complicated as it might seem. The most practical way is to use a standard bow net. The net can be set on top of the hack house and fresh meat tied down in the center of its arc. When the birds come down to eat — which they will eventually do — the net can be tripped. Its mesh does not injure a hawk. It is a good idea to trap one bird when the other is away hunting. The sight of a comrade being taken, struggling in the net, might be unsettling.

As I said, this hacking procedure is a time-honored method of raising and training young hawks to flight and hunting. But not many beginning North American falconers have the space or the time to utilize it. For those of you who do, fine. The rest of you will have to settle on other methods of teaching your hawk to fly and hunt.

10

Training and Flying
the Merlin/Pigeon Hawk

NOW THAT THE threat of DDT has passed in North America, it is possible for novice falconers — equipped with a permit — to both take eyas merlins from the nest and to trap wild birds.

Our merlin — of which there are four subspecies in this country — is a chunky, beautiful little falcon that subsists almost entirely on small songbirds. Each spring, the horde of songbirds move north to summer nesting areas and are followed by the merlins and the accipiter version of it, the sharp-shinned hawk. These hawks nest at the northern extremes of their migration. Then, in late summer, following the southward migration of their staple diet, the songbirds, the hawks head south.

The merlin is about the same size as the falcon kestrel and the female of the sharp-shinned hawk but is a much more compact, chunky falcon and weighs considerably more than the two others.

The European merlin nested almost exclusively on cliffs and rocks of the moors, so the Old World falconry literature seems to be talking about a different hawk. But it is the same bird as our pigeon hawk — although our merlin nests in pine trees. It will nest, occasionally, in an abandoned flicker hole in a dead tree, but most times the nests are found in conifers. Pigeon hawks will, if able, adopt old hawk, owl, and crow nests. They nest slightly later than most other hawks—perhaps because they tend to range far to the north and are found at high altitudes in the West and Northwest and in the Great Plains. The eggs are not laid until the first of June in many areas, and the young do not fly until early August. Pigeon hawks do not present as great a problem for the falconer seeking young from the nest as do the prairie falcons.

Like the sparrow hawk, the merlin is a noisy and demonstrative little hawk when it frequents a nesting area. Both parent birds will set up a clatter if an intruder gets too close to the nest. They do not attack —at least I have never heard of one attacking anyone—and will quietly leave when a climber gets to a nest.

They are a pretty hawk and quite easy to train. The female will weigh about 7½ ounces and the male about 1½ ounces less at the same stage. I cannot think of any aspect of their training that would be different from that of training kestrels, except perhaps that they have a tendency to make off with meat or game or "carry" more than the sparrow hawks.

Nest of the pigeon hawk is most likely to be in a conifer.

Heinz Meng swings a lure to exercise a falcon.

A trained merlin makes a very good hunter on small to medium-sized birds. It is strong of wing and very courageous. It hunts with a verve and style that is a pleasure to watch. Strangely enough, merlins exhibit a lot of the hunting traits of both the goshawk and the Cooper's hawk—flying low over the ground and whipping and twisting about in heavy cover after game. They are the only falcon I know that will pursue birds right into thickets and around tree trunks in heavy timber.

I had a female pigeon hawk in the late 1950s while living in the small community of Corrales, just north of Albuquerque, New Mexico, in the Rio Grande Valley. I had trapped it in a bow net during the fall migration. It was a big, strong bird for a merlin and would hunt practically any bird smaller than itself.

At one point, I found a small covey of Gambel quail in the willow and Russian olive thickets close to the banks of the Rio Grande. The merlin, after the first few futile flights for them in the thicket, learned to take them in the open field as they made for the cover. She would not climb above them and make a dive—as would a prairie falcon. Instead, she flew straight after them—zigzagging just above the streaking quail. Usually she would grab one just before it reached the cover and would ride it down like a goshawk—clutching as she went.

She was a fierce little bird, and I have seldom seen a better hunter. Sometimes she would streak past a speeding quail or meadowlark and, at the last instant, flare up in a quick turn and dive in perhaps a 5-foot stoop onto the bird—falling to the ground with it. As I said earlier, she had a tendency to carry while being trained, and it was sometimes necessary to sit down on the ground beside her—showing her meat on the glove—until she calmed down.

Her first reaction, always, was to cover the game with her wings and tail and, if startled, try to drag it under the shelter of a bush. Outside of this, she was an excellent falcon in the field.

11

The Prairie Falcon

SINCE THE ADVENT of DDT, and the making of the peregrine falcon a protected bird in the United States, the prairie falcon has come to be the most available large falcon in the U.S. Prairie falcons weigh just a bit less than a tundra peregrine, the males averaging about 1 pound and the females 1½ to 2 pounds.

They are a spectacularly beautiful falcon—with the crown, the face, and the entire topside of the hawk a sandy brown to slate color. The top feathers are edged with a buff color and the bars a slightly darker color. The tail is a slatey color with a white tip.

Primary feathers are a dark slate color spotted with white. The underwings are a pale buff to white. The throat is white, and a black line extends down from the eye to the white throat. The underparts are a creamy white streaked on the breast with dark brown darts. The cere and the feet are a bright yellow and the eyes brown.

Flying—as a silhouette—the prairie falcon can be easily mistaken for a peregrine. I've made the mistake a number of times as a prairie falcon streaks across the western sky late in the afternoon. After you look at enough prairie falcons, you become aware that the head is a bit larger and the tail a slight bit longer in relation to the body than is true of a peregrine. Sitting, the prairie falcon is not difficult to identify.

It can be found from Canada on the north down through the western and far western states to Mexico. It nests exclusively on cliffs in the west and breeds from New Mexico and Arizona north through Colorado and the rest of the western states to the Canadian border. It can be found at relatively high altitudes. I have found it breeding at 7,000 feet and higher in northern New Mexico. In 1949, I took two young prairie

Prairie falcon surveys the landscape from its block perch.

falcons from an aerie close to the top of a cliff in the gorge of the Rio Grande in northern New Mexico, north of Taos. It was not far from the top of the cliff, but the total drop to the river below was close to 1,000 feet and the experience was dizzying.

The prairie falcon is a magnificent hunter and a joy to watch in its natural state. During its migration, it kills mostly birds — the western meadowlark, the dove, and the prairie horned lark. But with the influx of starlings, pigeons and English sparrows to the West today, all three fall prey to this fleet falcon. In the spring, I have observed it feeding its young on prairie dogs, ground squirrels, chipmunks, and even the occasional burrowing owl. I found traces of skunk fur beneath one nest and bits of young badger near another. The nesting pair still take any number of birds during this time of the year, but I expect the mammals are easier to come by — particularly the young ones.

Through binoculars I have watched a pair of marauding prairie falcons set up prairie dogs for the kill. One will course back and forth over a stretch of ground close to a prairie dog town while the other circles far out and comes in low to the ground — always out of the sun. They will zoom in from the southeast in the early morning hours and from the southwest in late afternoon. It can be no mistake that they do this. Millions of years of hunting have taught them that ground mammals are vulnerable when squinting into the bright sunlight.

The prairie dogs will sit up on their mounds to watch one falcon dip and fly back and forth. They are easy prey for the other hawk streaking in at weed-top level. Sometimes the falcon will kill the rodent by clutching it, and other times it will knock it off its mound with a blow from a clenched fist as it whips by. It is going so fast at such times that when it passes by an observer, it makes a sound in the air like ripping cloth.

The prairie falcon is more ground-oriented than most other falcons found in North America. Its habitat is more like that of the gyrfalcon of the Arctic in that there is not so much ground cover in the wide open and arid West as in the Midwest, Far West, and East.

The prairie falcon, like the gyrfalcon on its tundra, is a bird of observation spots. It will take a position atop a telephone pole, rock outcropping, or lone tree until it spots prey. Then it makes a long, fast killing dive — usually ending in a flurry of flips and turns. While I've been dove hunting in the Southwest in September, I've had prairie falcons whip in from nowhere and take wounded doves from under my nose — literally. The mourning dove is one of the prairie falcon's favorite birds and the migrations of prey and predator coincide in early fall. As fast as the dove is, a prairie falcon can outfly and outmaneuver it.

The head of a prairie falcon, a creature whose natural tendency is to be some-what irascible and bad-tempered.

Not all prairie falcons make good hunting hawks. They are a bit irascible and bad-tempered by nature. Some will not gentle at all. Wild-trapped prairie falcons are notoriously difficult to tame down. I had some luck with one of the two I acquired in 1949 — the small male. Both gentled down after being taken from the nest, but the bigger female never seemed to get the hang of killing well. She made a rather nice pet and flew to a lure well, but she was a bit lazy — perhaps preferring meat from my glove to the effort of flying and killing. The tiercel, however, was a feisty little falcon. He declared war on the meadowlarks of the wide Rio Grande Valley north of Albuquerque and turned out to be a fine hunting hawk in the year I kept him. A big feral cat killed him on his block one afternoon while I was inside the house. The female was inside the mew at the time or the cat would have killed both.

Prairie falcons can be hacked very successfully if you have the room for it. They gentle down and train much the same as do the sparrow hawks and merlins — all being very much the same type of falcons. It is encouraging to see that the prairie falcon has been bred successfully in captivity — as has the peregrine. So there will be a readily available supply of domestically bred prairie falcons for some time to come — a reassuring thought for falconers.

12

Raising and Training the Short-Winged Hawks— Goshawk, Cooper's Hawk, and Sharp-Shinned Hawk

IN NORTH AMERICA today, a beginning falconer has a much better chance of getting a short-winged hawk than a falcon. These are the accipiters, and there are three in North America.

Biggest is the goshawk, a brawler of a hawk. The female weighs 2½ to 3½ pounds. The tiercel (male) of course weighs 1 to 1½ pounds.

The Cooper's hawk, the next smallest, looks a great deal like the bigger goshawk. The female weighs about 1 pound and the male 10 to 12 ounces.

The sharp-shinned is smallest of the three hawks. The female weighs about 9 to 10 ounces, the male several ounces less.

The big goshawk will take birds and mammals. The Cooper's and sharp-shinned are bird hawks. All three are hawks of the thick forests and heavy, brushy country. They hunt by stealth and swerve and dart between tree trunks to pursue their quarry right into thickets and brambles. They have short, stubby wings and long tails.

They can be identified easily in the air by their habit of flying with four or five quick wing beats and a glide. All are ferocious hunters and, when hungry or aroused, will attack anything up to their own size.

I first became acquainted with these hawks at Trailside Museum many years ago when we took them from nests and raised them for the falconry exhibit. As a teenager, I learned to build the bow perches for them and to fashion the jesses, hoods, and other gear. All three of the hawks can inflict considerable damage, and I spent much of my time extricating myself from their talons. Accipiters have a habit of lashing out with a talon whenever they are either hungry or angry, and it seemed they were always both.

The small sharp-shinned hawk is quite painful when it grabs you. The big goshawk's grip is awesome. Capable of killing a cock pheasant or a jackrabbit with ease, this hawk can inflict a terrible wound when it grasps your hand or arm. And the more you move, the harder a goshawk squeezes, its instincts telling it that its prey will cease to move the deeper it sinks in its talons.

You must pry open one talon at a time. In the process, considerable blood is lost. Because these hawks eat only meat — and bits lodge beneath skin and close to the base of talons — such a wound can fester very easily. It requires immediate medication.

These hawks are strictly the sprinters of falconry. They are very fast for short distances, but they won't go very far in pursuit of a quarry. Unlike the falcons, they hunt close to the ground. They kill by grasping and fastening onto their victims — repeatedly clenching their big talons until the quarry dies.

I have had a number of accipiters over the years, but I've really had hunting success with only the goshawk and several female Cooper's hawks.

I have tried the sharp-shinned — both male and female — and have found them marginal hunters. The male sharp-shinned hawk is really too small to be of use in hunting anything except songbirds, and that's illegal. Songbirds are protected. Sharp-shinned hawks tend to be very nervous and irritable. They are moody and will sulk when angry. They — like all the accipiters — need a lot of constant manning, unlike the falcons. The sharp-shinned hawk learns fast but will revert to an indifferent or wild state easily if not "maintained" all the time.

In some ways, the early training of the sharp-shinned hawk is much like that of the falcons, as far as the mew, the loft, and becoming accustomed to the falconer (or, in the case of accipiters, the "austringer") is concerned. Sharp-shinned hawks do not need to be hooded much. They gentle down more quickly if they can see around them. Also they have perching feet and need a bow perch or ring perch rather than a block perch on which to rest.

The big goshawk will take birds and mammals by pursuing them into thickets and brambles.

In the section on the falcons, I used the kestrel training as an example for all the falcons. Here, because the big goshawk is the most preferable of the three hawks for hunting, I will use its training methods as a basis for the two others. There is not a great deal of difference in the manner of training all three.

The goshawk is a northern hawk and a hawk of the higher elevations. It is not found much in the southern half of the United States. No matter where it is found, it usually is around pine forests. It does not necessarily nest in conifers, but it does seem to require the conifer forests to live in. I have found goshawk nests in the forks of elms and oaks in the Northeast, and in the forks of aspen trees in the mountains of the West. But these nesting trees were always surrounded by pines.

A goshawk is not hard to identify, although hawk fanciers I have known have sometimes mistaken it for the large white-gray gyrfalcon. When adult, the gos is a large gray hawk, with a black head, a white undertail covert, and a white streak over the eye. As an immature hawk, it is brown with dark-brown pencil marks on breast and undersides. The wings are evenly barred, as is the tail. The cere and the feet of the young and the adults are a greenish-yellow. The eyes of the young are a pale amber, turning to orange and later a dark red in adulthood. All three of the accipiters have a nervous habit of twitching their long tails and peering ferociously about them when perched on a limb.

The goshawk is a bloodthirsty hawk — a fact some modern naturalists seem to prefer to ignore. I don't know whether it's because they don't know or because many of today's young naturalists grew up in a school where they prefer to assume only man kills wantonly.

My associates and I at Trailside Museum knew better than to allow a goshawk to get free among the rest of the tethered hawks and owls. One would kill any number of them — not for food but simply for spite or outright rage. The goshawk will do the same thing in the wild. I have seen remains of ruffed grouse in the Northeast — killed by a pair of wintering goshawks near Kensico Lake in Westchester County, New York, left lying in the snow, uneaten. There would be another grouse not far away, in the same condition.

Goshawks will eat a victim if hungry, of course. But unlike any other hawk I know, they will sometimes kill for the sheer love of it. Old World falconry literature recognizes this habit of the goshawk. That fact makes its Latin name (*Accipiter gentilis*) even more ironic.

Taking young goshawks from a nest can be an interesting experience. The adults will often dive-bomb an intruder. People experienced in climbing to the nests of goshawks have learned to wear either a construction worker's hard hat or a football helmet. I received several skull scratches in the hardwoods of New England before learning this. Head-gear has stood me well in the West when I have climbed to the nests of these large, fierce hawks.

Wild-trapped goshawks make great hunters if they can be success-fully gentled to humans. I have had less success with this method than with raising them from eyas hawks. Perhaps it is because I have not trapped too many as passage birds. They are solitary hunters of the thick pine forests and woods, and it is more difficult to find them and trap them than it is the falcons.

When the eyas hawks are brought home, the same basic mew and loft is utilized as with the falcons. But a ring or bow perch should be used for the accipiters because of their huge gripping feet. A hood is not utilized nearly so much with these short-winged hawks as with falcons. The more they see and understand, the faster they tame down.

The main difference in handling accipiters as compared with fal-cons is that much more time is required in carrying them around on a glove. They need a great deal more exposure to *everything* – handling, carrying, feeding, stroking, people, dogs, light, cars, noises, and so on. In the beginning, it may be necessary to spend two to three hours a day with your goshawk. And the same thing is true of a Cooper's and sharp-shinned hawk.

Don't let too many people or dogs get close to your hawk at first or it will bate repeatedly from the fist. Keep people – when the gos has calmed down and will ride on the fist properly – on your right-hand side, where the hawk can see them at all times. Remember that an accipiter spends almost all its time while hunting on the fist of the aus-tringer (falconer).

Unlike the falcons, which soar above and wait on a falconer and his dog, the accipiter will launch its attack on flushing prey directly from the gloved fist. Walking it a great deal when gentling it down gets it accustomed to the motion of the falconer's walk and the movement of the glove. When not being carried, it should be left on its perch in a darkened room or on a screened perch.

A very important step in the accipiter's training is the one in which it learns to jump or fly from a perch or from a post to the falconer's fist. A few weeks after the beginning of its training, the goshawk should be flying several yards to the fist. Each time, it is offered food as a reward so that – *always* – there is that encouragement to return to the glove. By now the goshawk should be allowed to sit on its perch in full daylight.

A goshawk will fly to a lure on the ground, or one being dragged on the ground, but it will not stoop to a lure. Neither will any of the other accipiters. Their training consists almost entirely in your getting the hawk to fly from some other place to your fist. The idea is to make that distance longer each day until hawk is flying quickly to falconer across a yard or from a distance of 50 to 100 yards.

When the hawk will fly to your fist from such a distance, take off the leather leash and fasten a creance (long line) to the swivel at the end of the jesses. The hawk should fly as though it were not tethered. I use 12-pound-test monofilament line on a goshawk. Such line is strong and has enough elasticity to prevent its snapping. It is also light enough so that the hawk does not feel the weight. To the far end of the line, I tie a stick about a foot long — in case the hawk does try to fly away. The stick will drag and finally hang up on something.

It is pretty difficult to imitate the ear-piercing shriek of a goshawk when you call the bird to fist. I have no trouble imitating the calls of kestrels and the *cac, ca, ca, ca* of other falcons. But the accipiters are hard to copy. Since the falconer should make some sound when calling a shortwing hawk to the fist, I use a dog whistle. It works well.

A goshawk, at a certain stage of its training, is ready to hunt. A falconer who knows the accipiters will notice this stage. The hawk develops a look in its eye and a habit of clenching its feet on the glove. It begins to fly off the fist at all sorts of objects. It will have slimmed down to its "fighting weight." By weighing your hawks each day at the same time and while it is wearing the same equipment, you will be able to monitor the correct flying weight. A reasonable weight for a female gos to be flying well is just a little over 2 pounds.

Lots of red, lean beef will keep a goshawk in good condition. I have found that an occasional teaspoonful of cod-liver oil, mixed with the meat, keeps plumage in good shape. I smash up rabbit bones and fur with the meat to form the casting required by all hawks. The feathers of starlings and sparrows and some game birds, plus the heads, are also good food for goshawks. Be sure to feed all the goshawk's food to it either on the fist or the lure. That is where they are supposed to find it.

Female goshawks will take almost anything that flushes — including household cats and small dogs. So beware what you flush. Fortunately, we have no shortage of rabbits in North America — cottontails, that is. Both the male and female goshawk will take a cottontail readily, the big female dispatching it easily. I have had a few hawks discouraged as a result of their attacking jackrabbits in the West. The big female goshawk can usually handle one, provided she gets several talons on the head and another couple in the rear. But if the hawk fastens to the rear and gets dragged, the jack can deliver a tremendous series of kicks. A tiercel gos seldom wins that battle, and even a few females swear off jacks after a few bad bouts.

Start your gos off on rabbits. A male will take birds of any kind, usually, plus cottontails, squirrels, chipmunks, prairie dogs, and the like. But a lot of big females don't care much for birds. They will take pheasants, coots, and the occasional puddle duck that has to jump straight up to gain flying speed. But they will almost always take cottontail rabbits.

If they have trouble catching cottontails at first — as eyas training hawks — kill a rabbit, fasten a string to it, and hide it in cover. Have someone drag it out into the open, and the hawk will make a "kill" on it. Be sure to reward the hawk with fresh rabbit meat for its triumph. After that, it should have no trouble with killing rabbits.

Squirrels are good quarry for the goshawk, but they must be sighted on open ground where there are not too many trees. For that matter, ground squirrels are better than the eastern gray squirrel. The big gray, before it dies, can deliver a nasty bite to the legs of a hawk, so I quit hunting mine on them.

Hunting pheasants with a big female goshawk is the ultimate sport for me with these big accipiters. A pheasant is never far from dense cover when it lands, and many a time I have had a gos go right into the cover with the pheasant — holding onto it or right after it in "hot pursuit." A pheasant is a smart bird, and sometimes it takes three or more flushes from thick cover for the hawk to catch the big game bird. Hen pheasants are far easier for the goshawks to catch than the big cock birds.

Any good bird dog can be taught to hunt with a falcon or a short-winged hunting hawk. Also, almost any hawk that will hunt well can learn to work with a good dog. Hawk and dog develop a respect for each other. I think a pointing dog gives hunter and hawk a better chance to get ready for a flush. But I have also hunted hawks with Labrador retrievers and have had good luck.

Chuck Keene, a fine falconer at Cornwall-on-Hudson Museum in New York State, hunts ducks with a Lab and a female gos. He says the ducks don't know which way to go. If they fly, the gos gets them. If they dive under the surface of a pond to escape the hawk, the Lab will dive after them until they flush.

The Cooper's hawk and the sharp-shinned hawk can be trained just about the same way that a goshawk can, but both are more difficult to train. They have a tendency to be undependable and nervous. Only the female of the sharp-shinned hawk is worth training, and at times I think the male Cooper's hawk is a bit small for anything but starlings. I have found that the smaller of the accipiters do not do as well on beef as they do on birds and mice. Lots of sparrows, starlings, and chopped-up mice seem to keep them more healthy.

13

Releasing a Hawk
to the Wild

THERE WILL BE times when a hawk just does not develop well and seems certain never to make a good falcon. Some hawks are psychopaths.

Some young birds seem never able to get the hang of training. There are wild-trapped hawks that simply do not gentle to man. They spend their entire time in captivity trying to escape.

At any rate, there are a number of reasons a hawk might be freed. If you will take one out to release, keep several things in mind. Beforehand, all fellow falconers in the area should be notified. They may not have any real interest in the event, but the announcement is still a good idea. At least they may be able to keep some track of the bird after release.

I would follow regulations and notify the game-department authorities in my area if I intended to release a hawk. It is just possible the hawk might land in a yard or close to a residence and be either recaptured or injured. It would help the game men to know where it came from.

In the case of birds that have not yet learned to kill for themselves, they should be released only when well-fed. In addition, it is a good

Any of a number of reasons might cause a falconer to release a hawk to the wild. The move needs to be planned carefully.

idea to make some provisions to put food out for them for days after their release. You should return the next day to where the hawk was released and — if the bird was trained to a lure — swing a lure there. If the bird is accustomed to feeding on the fist, the falconer should go there with meat on a glove. These hawks might feed this way for several days before learning how to fend for themselves.

The weather is an important factor. Don't release hawks to the wild when it is unseasonably cold or rainy. High winds will blow young birds for a considerable distance. Even if they wanted to continue feeding on a lure, they could not.

14

Regaining a Lost Hawk

IT HAS BEEN a tragic thing to lose a falcon or a short-wing hawk any-time, but it's even more so today, with hawks so difficult to come by. But a good many hawks are recovered — especially falcons — if the right procedures are followed.

A falcon will return to a lure far longer than will the accipiters. An accipiter tends to get more nervous the longer it is free. Two or three nights out in the wild are all it needs to revert to the feral state. So it's best to get after one quickly and do your best in the first few hours.

The reasons that hawks escape are numerous. The most common one is ignorance on the part of a new falconer or austringer about the habits of hawks. Newcomers are not familiar with the bating practices of hawks and don't expect them to fly suddenly when they do. Begin-ning falconers tend to be careless with doors and windows in the mew and loft. And probably worst of all, they're often careless with knots.

Another reason hawks get away these days is that metal swivels are many times used instead of knots, and these swivels will sometimes mal-function. Then, many times a hawk will simply fly away while hunting or flying to the lure. If the hawk is fastened by a creance (light line), it will drag this line and the attached stick until it hangs up someplace and will be recovered. But if the hawk is flying free after game and takes off, it may go some distance. At least it is not encumbered with a leash which will certainly hang up and eventually cause the hawk to hang upside down and die. If an escaped hawk has a leash attached, all efforts should be made to recapture the hawk. Falconry already has enough enemies in the "protectionist" area of the outdoors. We shouldn't give them any example they might use to claim that falconry is a "cruel" sport to birds of prey.

I have lost a number of hawks over the years—in both the East and West. Most of them were recovered, but a few were lost. Most of the lost hawks were short-wing hawks. I can remember losing one peregrine from Trailside. Somehow it worked loose from the knots at its block and flew off over the Hudson River. We never saw it again, even though we looked for weeks.

Recovering a lost falcon from a tree.

Most of the Cooper's hawks and sharp-shinned hawks that I have failed to recover simply preferred the wild state to captivity. They would not decoy back to a lure or the fist. Migration times also played a part in their wanting to leave.

If a hawk gets away in wind, look downwind a long way for it. Watch for the action of crows in the East, magpies in the West. If a hawk gets away in thick cover, look and listen for the sounds of jays, wrens, and other songbirds. It may have made a kill and be crouched over it — causing much comment from the native birds.

An accipiter shakes its tail frequently — a lot when eating. For that reason, a tail bell is a must for a goshawk and I think also for big female Cooper's hawks. This type of bell is fastened to the base of the tail, as near center as possible. It can be heard a long way in heavy cover when a hawk is feeding.

A falcon or one of the long-wing hawks may fly about for a while after getting away. It will most likely land in a tree. Try offering it food from both the lure and the glove. That offer should bring it down. If it does not, and you either have another falcon or know another falconer who does, bring the other hawk up and begin flying it to a lure. Falcons are jealous birds, and that action should bring the escaped hawk to you in short order. It's smart to have two lures handy in case it does come back. You don't want two hawks squabbling over the same lure.

I've had to stay out until dark with a few hawks. They — falcons, that is — don't come to a glove or a lure too well when the light begins to fade. They'll go to roost in a tree at darkness. Then it is up to the falconer to climb up (or hire a spry youngster to do it) with a light flashlight, and slip a line through the hole in the jesses. Then the hawk can be taken down carefully. It might not be a bad idea to hood it before trying to carry it down, in case it bates in the branches and gets a few feathers battered.

With the short-wing hawks it can be a whole other scenario. They sulk, they grow moody, they flit from tree to tree, glaring and shaking their tails all the while. Sometimes they pay no attention to the lure or the meat on the glove. The only thing to do with these recalcitrant hawks is to stay with them until dark.

An accipiter will sometimes fly to the glove or lure just before dark — unlike the falcons. It may be because they are accustomed to hunting in dark forests and like to partake of a last meal before settling in for the night. The waning light seems to remind them it's time to eat.

There is always that hawk that won't stay in one tree. You lose sight of it in the dark. The only thing to do is to go home and get to bed early. Set your alarm clock so you'll be up early — before first light.

Sometimes a hawk will come down to the meat on the glove or lure the first thing in the morning. Hunger will be in your favor.

European falconers formerly used a system called "winding up" a hawk that would not stay on the lure when the falconer approached it. A peg was driven into the ground near the hawk, and the creance (light line) was fastened to it. Then the falconer, holding the creance, would walk slowly around the hawk at some distance while it stood on the lure.

If the falconer was lucky, the hawk did not spook at the feel of the light line close to its legs. If it still did not let the falconer approach, the loops of the creance were slowly drawn up until its legs were snared. Then, making sure the hawk did not panic, the falconer slowly picked the bird up and returned it to the gloved fist.

In cases where a hawk wouldn't come down to the fist or lure at all, a harness was placed on a live pigeon and the bird was tethered out where the hawk could see it. The falconer, after making sure the hawk was caught in the nylon loops, could retrieve both the hawk and the harness.

If a falconer does not have a pigeon harness, a pigeon can be tied in the center of a bow net and the net sprung when the hawk comes to kill and feed.

In this modern day of electronics, it is not at all surprising that a light and portable radio receiver is available for falconers. It can easily be carried by a falconer and consists of a receiver, antenna, and headset. Small, lightweight radio transmitters can now be fastened to the leg of a hawk. These devices are capable of transmitting a strong signal as far as 8 to 10 miles.

When a hawk carrying one of these transmitters is lost, the falconer simply gets out his sophisticated gear and heads into the field where the hawk was last seen. By turning the directional antenna until he picks up the signal, the falconer can simply follow the signal toward the lost hawk until it is located. This equipment is expensive, and a beginning falconer might not want to spend the money for such gear. But it is available.

15

Care and Treatment
of Hawks

A HAWK — YES, even a big, wild female goshawk — is in many ways a fragile creature. It is a highly efficient killing and flying machine that needs care and constant maintenance.

You need to remember that a hawk's feathers must be kept in good shape if it is to be a healthy bird and successfully flown at the lure and at game in the field. This is why so much care has gone into the designing of perches, jesses, and leashes over the centuries. A broken wing, foot, or feathers can make a falcon useless as a hunter.

Unlike most birds, falcons and accipiters cannot be kept in wire or screen cages. They will fly directly at the wire, probably thinking they can go through it. After finding they cannot, they will then grasp the wire or screen with their talons and try to climb it, resting on their tail feathers and breaking them off gradually. A hawk without tail feathers is like an aircraft without the vertical and horizontal stabilizer or "tail." It cannot be controlled in flight. The ends of the heavy primary wing flight feathers will also become broken and ragged from beating against a cage.

These healthy falcons show no hunger or shock traces.

In the handling of a newly acquired bird, be very careful to keep it from injury in any way. I have seen many a goshawk and Cooper's hawk break tail feathers in the first few days of captivity when not handled properly. Sometimes—particularly in getting a hawk accustomed to the block or perch—it helps to slip a small clear-plastic bag over the tail feathers and tape the top firmly to the base of the bird's spine (on top). By the time the hawk has calmed down, the feathers will still be in good shape.

The condition of many birds shipped by mail-order houses is a disgrace. A feather will break at its weakest point, a spot marked by a white streak. We call these hunger streaks. Although Webster grants they may be caused by periods of severe hunger, he also calls them "shock traces," believing they might have been caused by trauma. I am inclined to agree, because the appearance of many of the streaks coincides with such a traumatic experience as removal from the nest. Nevertheless, many hawks shipped by certain commercial establishments have been literally starved. Fortunately, such places are gradually being forced out of business.

I shall always remember one red-tailed hawk we managed to keep alive at Trailside Museum. It had been brought to us by someone who found it in a farmer's chicken yard. Apparently the bird had been shot nearby and had survived a broken wing. The farmer, probably just to see what would happen, had tossed the bird into the chicken yard with the rest of the fowl. It was an immature bird and probably had never killed anything bigger than a mouse or squirrel. It lived in that chicken yard for more than six months, feeding on the same grain the chickens ate.

That hawk was an unbelievable sight when brought to us. It was almost pure white, the hunger streaks making up almost the entire color of the wing and body. Its feet were gnarled from hopping and walking on them and because of a protein deficiency. The wing, which never healed properly, had to be dragged along. I thought it was a chicken. It would hop about the museum grounds on its crippled feet, peeping like a young chick when it was hungry, following us anywhere for food.

As pitiful as it was to those of us who knew and raised hawks, this tame bird was quite lovable. Everyone grew fond of the bird. Under the direction of Bill Carr, the museum chief (who now lives in Tucson, Arizona, and heads the Sonora Desert Museum under the auspices of the Pack Foundation), we managed to get it back into decent shape after a few months. It grew feathers each year, as most birds would, and it lived a number of years at the museum on a diet of fresh meat, fur, feathers, and cod liver oil.

The mending of broken feathers is called imping. It's a technique that in some ways has been improved because of the marvelous epoxy glues on the market. On the other hand, it has become hard to find feathers to replace those broken. In years past, a falconer could borrow feathers from fellow falconers, buy them in a dozen places, or just save feathers from his molting hawks. But if a modern-day falconer is lucky enough to have a single hawk, he is doubly lucky to find any spare flight feathers or tail feathers.

The imping process is far easier than most old books would have you believe. The broken feather is neatly cut. Note: Only the shaft, not the feathers, is cut, with sharp scissors. It should be cut about halfway up, where the shaft is the largest and strongest. The feather to be substituted should, if possible, be the same length and size as the one broken. Bamboo slivers, light and strong, have been used for ages as imping needles. They can hardly be improved upon as connecting rods, although metal is available today that does the job well. Bobby pins make good imping needles because they are flat and do not have a tendency to loosen or turn. The needle should be cut about an inch long and each end filed to a sharp point. Dip the needle in any of the new fast-drying and unbelievably strong epoxy glues, insert it in the two sections of the feather shafts, and gently and carefully fit together the shafts. I prefer to do this operation while the hawk is hooded. It will not panic and will usually submit to gentle handling since no pain is involved. Some modern falconers advocate tranquilizers for hawks when major repair work is needed on flight feathers. But considering the value of a hunting hawk today, I would prefer not to gamble on drugging one!

Accipiters, by the way, are more likely than falcons to break flight feathers since they dive directly into thick brush after game.

Sudden loss of feathers in your new hawk is no cause for alarm. Hawks molt each year. Although I have had several that did not have a complete molt, generally all the flight feathers will come out and be replaced each year. Young birds taken from the nest, as well as immature or passage hawks, will usually molt more easily the next year than older haggard hawks, which do not always molt completely on schedule. The molt (as in many other wild species of birds, such as waterfowl) occurs in the spring and summer when the birds need to fly less than in fall and winter to catch food. Nature thought of all such nifty arrangements millions of years ago.

A hawk can be brought successfully through its molt each year on the perch if the falconer wishes. But fewer feathers are broken if the bird is placed in a quiet room away from distractions. Some falconers simply leave the hawk to itself during the molt and place its food inside

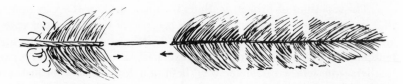

Imping process involves cutting shaft of damaged feather, then adding imping needle with epoxy glue and section of replacement feather. This replacement section shows hunger or shock traces.

the quiet room. I prefer to take it on the fist and feed it at least twice a day — to keep up that hawk–human relationship I consider so important. The hawk does not forget its training if put in a quiet room during molt, but it is pleasant to renew its acquaintance each day.

Now we come to an area — what to do about sick hawks — in which there is considerable room for discussion. Much can be learned from old books on falconry, but I prefer to follow some standard practices of modern veterinary medicine. In cases of extremely ill falcons or accipiters, consult a veterinarian, particularly one familiar with poultry diseases.

The hawks I've raised have had few ailments. The most common is a tendency for the bird to become listless and for its mute (droppings) to change from white to green. Our cure for this has always been freshly killed game, fed to the bird with feathers and/or fur attached, to provide the roughage needed for a bird of prey to cast up a pellet. The meat is digested and passed into the stomach, while feathers, bits of bone, and fur separate from the meat in the crop of the bird and later are cast up as this pellet. In some cases, where fur or feathers are not available (although it is hard to imagine a place where a falconer might not be able to trap mice), small pieces of untreated rope can be shredded up with the meat to be cast up later. Cod-liver oil mixed with lean meat and roughage has cured many a sick and listless hawk for us. A hawk should be fed roughage at least once a week.

The best way to prevent disease in hawks is to keep its surroundings clean. It is essential to change worn and greasy jesses and leashes and to scour perches. All meat eaters tend to leave bits of food about. Anyone who has climbed to a hawk's nest on a ledge or in a tree can testify to that. Contrary to some belief, hawks will feed on rotten meat in the wild and do not always eat only what they have just killed. Distantly related to vultures, they sometimes show the same traits. Certainly our

A woman's nylon stocking surrounds hawk and holds it while falconer hoods it.

noble national emblem, the bald eagle, is no purist. It is a scavenger, and its main diet is dead fish.

Hawks get colds like anybody else, usually from dampness and drafts. One old cure that seems to work is to feed the bird some boiled-down rhubarb solution with an eye dropper. It may fall under the heading of a folk-medicine cure-all, but it does seem to help. A good bird vet, however, will have many new medicines that cure both colds and coughs in hawks.

Frounce, a particularly virulent form of disease appearing in hawks, is contracted from the eating of pigeons. It appears as a yellowish growth in the mouth, usually accompanied by green coloration in the mutes and listless eating. The hawk may tear off meat and fling it about the perch. Since this disease can be fatal in a few weeks, contact a vet quickly. It is treated with a drug called enheptin, which can be purchased from a vet or a pharmacist and should be carried on trips in case no vet is available. It comes in capsules that can be concealed inside a piece of fresh meat, which the hawk should swallow whole. If it does not, force-feed it. A week of this treatment should begin to cure the problem. Wait another week and then repeat the process the third week. The drug also helps to prevent recurrence of the disease.

Frounce is said to be caused, in many cases, by the protozoon in fresh pigeon flesh. But it has been said by some falconers and vets that if the pigeon is allowed to cool after killing it, the organism dies before it can infect a hawk.

Aspergillosis, a lethal ailment in hawks, is caused by molds that infect the lungs of birds of prey. It affects hawks from the extreme north more than others. Difficult to diagnose, it can be spotted by only a very experienced falconer or vet. There are a number of treatments — such as the antibiotics amphoteracin and eucilin — but these, too, should be administered only by a vet.

Coccidiosis, a disease well known in poultry, occurs in hawks. It usually shows up as spots of red in droppings. That is about the only symptom until the mutes turn blackish and the bird becomes listless. It will die if not treated by a vet.

Cramp, a crippling of the feet, occurs mostly in young birds. It is thought to occur because the eyases were chilled after they were taken from the nest. There is no known cure.

Egg yolk is rich in vitamin A and can be used to feed hawks during the moult. It keeps the cere and the legs a bright, healthy yellow color. The moult in hawks starts about March or April and generally takes about five months to completely replace all the feathers. During this time, the hawk is placed in the mew, leash and bells are removed, and jesses are oiled to keep them soft. The hawk should be offered a bath several times a week and fed regularly. I like to feed hawks twice a day on the fist during moult — just to keep them familiar with the falconer. There are some medicines that are fed to hawks to shorten the moult, but there is not much you can do with hawks in the late spring and summer — as far as hunting them is concerned — and it seems to me unnecessary to shorten the moult.

Most hawks will show signs if they become ill. Usually, if a hawk is healthy, it will preen itself regularly, bathe, shake itself to arrange its feathers, stretch both legs and wings regularly, cross its wings behind itself, and wipe its beak on the perch after meals. Its eyes are round and shiny, its weight will remain constant, and it will sleep comfortably on one leg. If it shows signs of sluggishness, loses weight, or flips away pieces of its meat, or if its mutes show signs of blood or tinges of green, or if its castings or pellets are watery and misshapen, have your hawk looked at by a vet.

Internal parasites may occur in hawks, but that condition is usually the fault of unclean mews or of a hawk's being run down and in poor shape. This is called capillariasis, and the only well-known drug for it is one called thiabendazole — given with the hawk's food. Consult a vet. External parasites usually can be handled by anti-parasitic powder.

The gapeworm, a parasite common to poultry, now and then affects hawks. It is also treated by thiabendazole, but better let the vet do it.

Tapeworms now and then show up in hawks, and some vets recommend tetrachlorethylene.

A watery blister has been known to show up on the wing joints of hawks. This malady usually requires the lancing of the blister and its treatment with a mild disinfectant until it heals.

Heat and direct sunlight are the most likely causes of death in hawks. Never leave a hawk in the hot sunlight for any length of time, and be careful that a room does not become overheated.

I remember being concerned years ago about parasites in my hawks, but no longer. Internal parasitic infections picked up by eating rodents and some birds can be treated with drugs by a vet. Intestinal worms these days can be easily and quickly flushed from hawks. The once-dreaded intestinal roundworm, as well as other parasites, can be removed by treatment with piperazine salts — again administered by a vet.

Lice infest the feathers of most hawks. They do no real harm, feeding on the skin powder of the birds of prey. Fairly large flat flies, they can be removed with a light sprinkle of derris dust.

I remember my first surprise on finding the ears of hawks sometimes filled with maggots. This happens a great deal in the wild, probably starting in the nest. I have found maggots mostly in young birds, particularly in the buteo or slow-flying hawks. We picked the maggots out with tweezers years ago, but now with an eyedropper we simply put a few drops (in the ears) of any nondetergent light oil. Baby oil does well.

Sometimes a hawk will just get bored to death. This is particularly so of the fierce goshawk. For a hawk to remain interested and alert, it should be kept someplace where it can see people regularly. Dogs, moving vehicles, adults, young children — all can be in the area, so long as they don't have too great an access to the hawk. A hawk is curious and active. If left alone, it will get sick and die. And the accipiters require more hustle and bustle about them than do the falcons.

Most hawks enjoy baths. Since they tend to take an occasional drink from the bath water, it is best to change it each day. I suggest using a wide but shallow pan, without sharp edges that can cut a foot. And the water, depending upon the size of the hawk, can be anywhere from a few inches to six or eight inches deep. I have seen hawks bathe in water up to their shoulders, and I have seen others that hated water and never took a bath.

Keep a watch on the hawk's beak and talons. Sometimes the point of the beak gets too long and too sharp from not eating enough tough food and not cracking the bones of game. Immobilize the hawk by slipping a stocking over it, and carefully pare back the beak to its original shape. Do not splinter any of the beak in the process. Talons may grow too long because of a soft perch and not enough rubbing on stones — a general lack of use. Cut off the sharp tips with a nail cutter, being careful not to crack or splinter them.

Some caution must be taken about providing water for hawk baths. Two or three times a week is about the right frequency to offer bath water in the summer or hot weather — less in cold weather. Don't offer a hawk a bath on cold, rainy days or late in the day. A wet hawk will sit on its perch or block in the darkness, and there is always the danger of its catching cold. If a hawk gets wet by accident late in the day or is drenched by a late rain shower, let an electric light bulb burn near it that night. Hawks will dry out their feathers before going to sleep.

One thing to remember about feeding a hawk with a hood on is not to feed a casting to a hawk wearing a Dutch hood. This type of hood prevents a hawk from regurgitating a pellet. A hawk is liable to choke itself if it tries to get rid of a pellet while wearing this type of hood. An Indian-type hood does permit a hawk to pass a pellet.

There are a few things to learn about putting on and taking off a hood. The hood is put on a hawk to keep it from becoming excited and flying off at random when first brought home. It immobilizes a hawk the moment it is in place, and the bird may be moved about on the fist, on a cadge, or in a car, train or airplane. A hood also comes in handy to put on other hawks that may be waiting their turn to fly — either at game or a lure.

There is a right and a wrong way to put on a hood. It should not be pushed on a hawk, and the back of a hawk's head must not be thrust forward into the hood. No hawk should be handled so roughly that it might fall off the perch or wrist while being hooded, or it learns to dodge and twist as a hood is being put on.

The hood should be carried upside-down in the falconer's right hand as the hawk rests on the gloved left hand. The hood is held by the base of the plume and brought up slowly almost against the hawk's breast. It should be slipped up and over a hawk's head with one single smooth movement.

A hood is equipped with four leather thongs in back. Two are used to close the hood and two to open it. When the hood is in place, the right hand takes hold of the outer closing thong of the hood and the left-hand thong is taken in the teeth of the falconer. Gentle pressure from both directions closes the hood straps and prevents the hawk from dislodging it by a shake of the head. The same technique is used to open the hood.

Weighing is by far the most important aspect of maintenance in the keeping of hunting hawks. Maintaining a correct "flying weight" is of the utmost importance. In the United States, it is quite easy to get a postage scale from most stationery stores. I prefer one that runs up to 3 pounds and is graduated in ½- and ¼-ounce increments — the ¼-ounce marks for small hawks and the ½-ounce marks for the bigger ones. These are relatively inexpensive scales — $10 to $20 — and worth every cent.

I drill small holes in the surface of the weighing plate and mount either a block for falcons or a section of stick for the perch of the shortwing hawks. They sit quietly after a few moments.

You must make certain the hawk is weighed at the same time each day and with the same equipment on (that is, jesses, bells, leash, hood, or whatever).

Moving a hawk about can bring up some interesting problems. Hawks, like falconers, get carsick and airsick. For that reason, while it is a good idea to feed a hawk well for several days before moving it, do not feed it on the day it is going to be transported. Also, it is best to move an adult hawk with its hood on. Young birds not trained to hoods can be transported and shipped in cardboard boxes to prevent feather damage. But remember, if a hawk is fed before being transported and is then hooded, it may throw up and choke itself inside the hood.

It might be wise to brace the inside of the cardboard box in which you transport the young hawks, to prevent it from being crushed in transit. Also, fastening burlap to the bottom gives the young hawks something to hang onto if the box is jostled.

A perch can easily be designed for the top of the back seat of a car or station wagon. I wrap canvas about a heavy dowel and tack it down. It gives hawks something into which they can sink their talons while riding. All hawks should be hooded while riding in cars.

If a hawk has trouble getting its weight down to a good flying level — usually after the long months of moult — try washed meat. It is an ancient remedy and works very well for reducing. Take long, thin strips of lean beef and soak them in cold, fresh water for 24 hours in the refrigerator. Wring out the juices until the meat is white, and feed it to overweight hawks. They may not take it readily because of the strange color, so it may have to be given to the bird with its hood on. Feed washed meat for about five days. You will notice a satisfactory drop in weight and a general improvement of the bird's condition.

16

New Federal
Falconry Regulations

(50 CFR 21)

§21.28 Falconry permits.

    (a) [Reserved]

    (b) *Permit requirements.* A falconry permit is required before any person may take, transport, or possess raptors for falconry purposes.

    (c) *Application procedures.*

        (1) An applicant who wishes to practice falconry in a State listed in §21.29(k) and which has been designated as a participant in a joint Federal/State permit system must submit an application for a falconry permit to the appropriate agency of that State. Each such application must incorporate a completed official form approved by the Service and must include all of the following information:

            (i) The number of raptors the applicant possesses at the time the application is submitted and the species, age (if known), sex (if known), date of acquisition, and source of each; and

        (ii) Any additional information required by the State to which the application is submitted.

    (2) An applicant who wishes to practice falconry in a State listed in §21.29(k) and designated as a non-participant in a joint Federal-State permit system must submit an application for a falconry permit to the Special Agent in Charge designated by §13.11(b) of this subchapter. Each such application must incorporate a completed official application form provided by the Service, and must include all of the following information:

        (i) The number of raptors which the applicant possesses at the time the application is submitted and the species, age (if known), sex (if known), date of acquisition, and source of each; and

        (ii) A statement as to whether the applicant has applied for a State falconry permit from a State listed in §21.29(k) of this subchapter and the name of the State and the date and file number of any application or other correspondence.

(d) *Issuance criteria.* Upon receiving an application completed in accordance with paragraph (c) of this section, the Director will decide whether a permit should be issued. In making his decision, the Director shall consider, in addition to the general criteria in §13.21(b) of this subchapter, the following factors:

    (1) Whether such action would have a significant effect on the wild population of raptors; and

    (2) Whether the Service and a State listed in §21.29(k) of this subpart concur that the applicant has met the appropriate requirements of State and Federal law and, in the case of a State listed in §21.29(k) as a participant in a joint Federal/State permit system, that a joint Federal/State permit should be issued or, in the case of a State listed in §21.29(k) as a non-participant in a joint Federal/State permit system, that separate permits should be issued by each authority.

(e) *Permit conditions.* In addition to the general conditions set forth in Part 13 of this subchapter, every permit issued under this section shall be subject to the following special conditions:

    (1) A permittee may not take, transport, or possess a golden eagle (*Aquila chrysaetos*) unless authorized in writing under §22.24 of this subchapter;

    (2) Any permittee may —

        (i) Transfer any raptor to another permittee if the transaction occurs entirely within a State and no money or other consideration is involved;

 (ii) Transfer any raptor to another permittee in an interstate transaction if the prior written approval of all State agencies which issued the permits is obtained and no money or other consideration is involved in the transaction; or

 (iii) Purchase, sell, or barter any lawfully possessed raptor which is bred in captivity under authority of a raptor propagation permit issued under §21.30 and banded with a numbered seamless marker issued or authorized by the Service, subject to the following additional conditions:

   (A) The person who receives any raptor by transfer, purchase, sale, or barter must be authorized to possess it under this part, or, if in a foreign country, must be authorized to receive it by the competent wildlife management authority of his/her country of residence or domicile after the competent wildlife management authority of that country has certified in writing that the recipient is an experienced falconer or raptor propagator who is required to maintain any raptors in his/her possession under conditions that are comparable to the conditions under which a permittee must maintain raptors under §21.29 or 21.30; and

   (B) The permittee who transfers, purchases, or sells, or barters any raptor must have acquired the raptor from a person authorized to possess it, and, if acquired from a person in the U.S., that person must be authorized to possess it under this part.

 (3) A permittee may not take, possess, or transport a raptor in violation of the restrictions, conditions, and requirements of §21.29 of this subpart; and

 (4) By July 31 of each year, a permittee shall submit a falconry report to the authority which issued the permit. A report shall contain the following:

  (i) A listing of all raptors in his possession on June 30 of the year in which the report is filed by species, marker number, sex (if known), age (if known), and date and where or from whom acquired.

(iii) A listing of all raptors possessed or acquired since the previous annual report, but no longer possessed, by species, marker number, sex (if known), age (if known), date and where or from whom acquired or given to, whether escaped, died, or released, and when the event occurred; and

(iii) Any other information required by the authority to which the report is submitted.

(f) *Duration of permits.* A permit or the renewal of a permit is valid when issued by the Service and expires on June 30 of the second calendar year after it is issued, unless a different period is specified on the permit or the renewal.

[41 FR 2238, Jan. 15, 1976; 48 FR 31608, July 8, 1983]

§21.29 Federal falconry standards.

(a) *General.* Under §21.28(d) of this subpart, a falconry permit will not be issued by the Service unless there is a joint concurrence in that decision by the Service and an appropriate official of a State listed in paragraph (k) of this section. A person who has obtained a valid falconry permit issued by the Service may take, possess and transport raptors for falconry in a State only in accordance with laws and regulations of that State, and he may not violate any of the minimum Federal standards, restriction, conditions, or requirements of this section even if not adopted by the State in question.

(b) *More restrictive State laws.* Nothing in this section shall be construed to prevent a State from making and enforcing laws or regulations not inconsistent with the standards contained in any convention between United States and any foreign country for the protection of raptors or with the Migratory Bird Treaty Act, and which shall give further protection to raptors.

(c) *Review and determination.* Any State may obtian a review and determination of its existing laws or regulations relating to falconry from the Director within 90 days by submitting a written request to that effect to the Director accompanied by a complete set of the laws and regulations relating to falconry, certified as complete, true and correct by the appropriate State official, and including sample permits. In order for the Director to make a determination that State laws or regulations meet Federal falconry standards, such laws or regulations must provide as a minimum those restrictions, conditions, and requirements contained in paragraphs (d) through (j) of this section.

When a determination is made that State laws or regulations meet or exceed these standards, notice will be published in the FEDERAL REGISTER and the State will be listed in paragraph (k) of this section.

(d) *Permit.* State laws or regulations shall provide that a valid State falconry permit from either that State or another State meeting Federal falconry standards and listed in paragraph (k) of this section is required before any person may take, possess, or transport a raptor for falconry purposes or practice falconry in that State.

(e) *Classes of permits.* States may have any number of classes of falconry permits provided the standards are not less restrictive than the following:

(1) *Apprentice (or equivalent) class.*

(i) Permittee shall be at least 14 years old;

(ii) A sponsor who is a holder of a General or Master Falconry Permit or equivalent class is required for the first two years in which an apprentice permit is held, regardless of the age of the permittee. A sponsor may not have more than three apprentices at any one time;

(iii) Permittee shall not possess more than one raptor and may not obtain more than one raptor for replacement during any 12-month period; and

(iv) Permittee shall possess only the following raptors which must be taken from the wild: an American kestrel (*Falco sparverius*), a red-tailed hawk (*Buteo jamaicensis*), a red-shouldered hawk (*Buteo lineatus*), or in Alaska only, a goshawk (*Accipiter gentilis*).

(2) *General (or equivalent) class.*

(i) A permittee shall be at least 18 years old;

(ii) A permittee shall have at least two years experience in the practice of falconry at the apprentice level or its equivalent;

(iii) A permittee may not possess more than two raptors and may not obtain more than two raptors for replacement birds during any 12-month period; and

(iv) A permittee may not take, transport, or possess any golden eagle or any species listed as threatened or endangered in Part 17 of this subchapter.

(3) *Master (or equivalent) class.*

(i) An applicant shall have at least five years experience in the practice of falconry at the general class level or its equivalent.

(ii) A permittee may not possess more than three raptors and may not obtain more than two raptors taken from the wild for replacement birds during any 12-month period.

(iii) A permittee may not take any species listed as endangered in Part 17 of this chapter, but may transport or possess such species in accordance with Part 17 of this chapter.

(iv) A permittee may not take, transport, or possess any golden eagle for falconry purposes unless authorized in writing under §22.24 of this subchapter;

(v) A permittee may not take, in any twelve (12) month period, as part of the three-bird limitation, more than one raptor listed as threatened in Part 17 of this chapter, and then only in accordance with Part 17 of this chapter.

(f) *Examination.* State laws or regulations shall provide that before any State falconry permit is issued the applicant shall be required to answer correctly at least 80 percent of the questions on a supervised examination provided or approved by the Service and administered by the State, relating to basic biology, care, and handling of raptors, literature, laws, regulations or other appropriate subject matter.

(g) *Facilities and equipment.* State laws or regulations shall provide that before a State falconry permit is issued the applicant's raptor housing facilities and falconry equipment shall be inspected and certified by a representative of the State wildlife department as meeting the following standards:

(1) *Facilities.* The primary consideration for raptor housing facilities whether indoors (mews) or outdoors (weathering area) is protection from the environment, predators, or undue disturbance. The applicant shall have the following facilities, except that depending upon climatic conditions, the issuing authority may require only one of the facilities described below.

(i) Indoor facilities (mews) shall be large enough to allow easy access for caring for the raptors housed in the facility. If more than one raptor is to be kept in the mews, the raptors shall be tethered or separated by partitions and the area for each bird shall be large enough to allow the bird to fully extend its wings. There shall be at least one window, protected on the inside by vertical bars, spaced narrower than the

        width of the bird's body, and a secure door that can
be easily closed. The floor of the mews shall permit
easy cleaning and shall be well drained. Adequate
perches shall be provided.

  (ii) Outdoor facilities (weathering area) shall be fenced
and covered with netting or wire, or roofed to protect the birds from disturbance and attack by predators except that perches more than 6½ feet high need
not be covered or roofed. The enclosed area shall be
large enough to insure the birds cannot strike the
fence when flying from the perch. Protection from
excessive sun, wind, and inclement weather shall be
provided for each bird. Adequate perches shall be
provided.

(2) *Equipment.* The following items shall be in the possession
of the applicant before he can obtain a permit or license:

  (i) Jesses — At least 1 pair of Alymeri jesses or similar type
constructed of pliable, high-quality leather or suitable synthetic material to be used when any raptor
is flown free. (Traditional 1-piece jesses may be used
on raptors when not being flown.);

  (ii) Leashes and swivels — At least 1 flexible, weather-resistant leash and 1 strong swivel of acceptable falconry design;

  (iii) Bath container — At least 1 suitable container, 2 to 6
inches deep and wider than the length of the raptor,
for drinking and bathing for each raptor;

  (iv) Outdoor perches — At least 1 weathering area perch
of an acceptable design shall be provided for each
raptor; and

  (v) Weighing device — A reliable scale or balance suitable
for weighing the raptor(s) held and graduated to increments of not more than ½ ounce (15 grams) shall
be provided.

(3) *Maintenance.* All facilities and equipment shall be kept at
or above the preceding standards at all times.

(4) *Transportation; temporary holding.* A raptor may be transported or held in temporary facilities which shall be provided with an adequate perch and protected from extreme
temperatures and excessive disturbance, for a period not
to exceed 30 days.

(h) *Marking.*

(1) State laws or regulations shall provide that an inventory

and description of all raptors held within that State, except those held for scientific or zoological purposes, shall be made and reported to that State within 90 days of the date when that State is listed in paragraph (k) of this section. This paragraph applies to all such raptors, whether or not the owner intends to submit an application for a falconry permit.

(2) State laws or regulations shall provide that no raptor may be acquired after the date when that State is listed in paragraph (k) of this section unless the person acquiring the raptor first obtains a numbered, non-reusable marker supplied by the Service, and attaches it to the raptor immediately upon acquisition.

(3) State laws or regulations shall also provide that the alteration, counterfeiting or defacing of a marker is prohibited except that permittees may remove the rear tab on markers and may smooth any imperfect surface provided the integrity of the marker and numbering are not affected.

(i) *Taking restrictions.* State laws or regulations shall provide the following restrictions on the taking of raptors from the wild:

(1) Young birds not yet capable of flight (eyasses) may only be taken by a General or Master Falconer during the period specified by the State and no more than two eyasses may be taken by the same permittee during the specified period.

(2) First-year (passage) birds may be taken only during the period specified by the State;

(3) In no case shall the total of all periods of taking of eyasses or passage birds exceed 180 days during a calendar year, except that a marked raptor may be retrapped at any time; and

(4) Only American kestrels (*Falco sparverius*) and great-horned owls (*Bubo virginianus*) may be taken when over one year old, except that any raptor other than endangered or threatened species taken under a depredation (or special purpose) permit may be used for falconry by General and Master falconers.

(j) *Other restrictions.* State laws or regulations shall provide the following restrictions or conditions:

(1) A person who possesses a lawfully acquired raptor before the enactment of these regulations and who fails to meet the permit requirements shall be allowed to retain the raptors. All such birds shall be identified with markers

supplied by the Service and cannot be replaced if death, loss, release, or escape occurs.

(2) A person who possesses raptors before the enactment of these regulations, in excess of the number allowed under his class permit, shall be allowed to retain the extra raptors. All such birds shall be identified with markers supplied by the Service and no replacement can occur, nor may an additional raptor be obtained, until the number in possession is at least one less than the total number authorized by the class of permit held by the permittee.

(3) A falconry permit holder shall obtain written authorization from the appropriate State wildlife department before any species not indigenous to that State is intentionally released to the wild, at which time the marker from the released bird shall be removed and surrendered to the State wildlife department. The marker from an intentionally released bird which is indigenous to that State shall also be removed and surrendered to the State wildlife department. A standard Federal bird band shall be attached to such birds by the State or Service-authorized Federal bird bander whenever possible.

(4) Another person may care for the birds of a permittee if written authorization from the permittee accompanies the birds when they are transferred: *Provided,* That if the period of care will exceed thirty (30) days, the appropriate State wildlife department shall be informed in writing by the permittee of this action within three (3) days of the transfer and informed where the birds are being held, the reason for the transfer, who is caring for them, and approximately how many days they will be in the care of the second person; and

(5) Feathers that are molted or those feathers from birds held in captivity that die, may be retained and exchanged by permittees only for imping purposes.

(k) *States Meeting Federal Falconry Standards.* In accordance with this section, the Director has determined that the following States meet or exceed the minimum Federal standards for regulating the taking, possession, and transportation of raptors for the purpose of falconry as set forth herein.

*Alabama	*Arkansas
*Alaska	*California
*Arizona	*Colorado

*Florida
*Georgia
*Idaho
*Illinois
*Indiana
*Iowa
*Kentucky
*Louisiana
*Maine
*Maryland
*Massachusetts
*Michigan
*Minnesota
*Mississippi
*Missouri
*Montana
*Nebraska

*Nevada
*New Jersey
*New Mexico
*New York
*North Carolina
*North Dakota
*Oklahoma
*Oregon
*Pennsylvania
*South Carolina
*South Dakota
*Texas
*Utah
*Virginia
*Washington
*Wisconsin
*Wyoming

[Note: States which are participants in a joint Federal/State permit system will be designated by an asterisk.] [41 FR 2238, Jan. 15, 1976; 41 FR 8053, Feb. 24, 1976, as amended at 42 FR 42353, Aug. 23, 1977; 43 FR 968, Jan. 5, 1978; 43 FR 10566, Mar. 14, 1978; 43 FR 34150, Aug. 3, 1978; 43 FR 57606, Dec. 8, 1978; 45 FR 25066, Apr. 14, 1980; 45 FR 70276, Oct. 23, 1980; 48 FR 31608, July 8, 1983]

§21.30 Raptor propagation permits.
  (a) *Permit requirement.* A raptor propagation permit is required before any person may take, possess, transport, sell, purchase, barter, or transfer any raptor, raptor egg or raptor semen for propagation purposes. The information collection requirements contained within this section have been approved by the Office of Management and Budget under 44 U.S.C. 3501 *et seq.* and assigned clearance number 1018-0022. This information is being collected to provide information necessary to evaluate permit applications. This information will be used to review permit applications and make decisions, according to the criteria established in this section for the issuance or denial of such permits. The obligation to respond is required to obtain or retain a permit.
  (b) *Application procedures.* Applications for raptor propagation permits must be submitted to the appropriate Special Agent in Charge (See §13.11(b) of this chapter). Each application must

contain the general information and certification required by
§13.12(a) of this chapter, plus the following additional information:

(1) A statement indicating the purpose(s) for which a raptor
propagation permit is sought and, where applicable, the
scientific or educational objectives of the applicant.

(2) A statement indicating whether the applicant has been
issued a State permit authorizing raptor propagation (include name of State, permit number, and expiration date);

(3) A statement fully describing the nature and extent of the
applicant's experience with raptor propagation or handling
raptors;

(4) A description of each raptor the applicant possesses or
will acquire for propagation purposes to include the species, age (if known), sex (if known), date of acqusition,
source, and raptor marker number;

(5) A description of each raptor the applicant possesses for
other than raptor propagation to include the species, age (if
known), sex (if known), date of acquisition, source, raptor
marker number, and purpose for which it is possessed.

(6) A description and photographs of the facilities and equipment to be used by the applicant including the dimensions
of any structures intended for housing the birds;

(7) A statement indicating whether the applicant requests
authority to take raptors or raptor eggs from the wild.

(c) *Issuance criteria.* Upon receiving an application completed in
accordance with paragraph (b) of this section, the Director
will decide whether a permit should be issued. In making this
decision, the Director shall consider, in addition to the general
criteria in §13.21(b) of this chapter, the following factors:

(1) Whether an applicant's raptor propagation facilities are
adequate for the number and species of raptors to be held
under the permit.

(2) Whether propagation is authorized by the State in which
the propagation will occur, and if authorized, whether the
applicant has any required State propagation permit.

(3) Whether the applicant is at least 18 years old with a minimum of 2 years experience handling raptors of the species
to be propagated, and if the applicant requests authority
to propagate endangered or threatened species, whether
the applicant is at least 23 years old with a minimum of
7 years experience handling raptors of the species to be
propagated.

(4) If the applicant requests authority to take raptors or raptor eggs from the wild—

    (i) Whether issuance of the permit would have a significant effect on any wild population of raptors;

    (ii) Whether suitable captive stock is available; and

    (iii) Whether wild stock is needed to enhance the genetic variability of captive stock.

(d) *Additional permit conditions.* In addition to the general conditions found in Part 13 of this chapter, raptor propagation permits are subject to the following additional conditions:

(1) *Facilities.* Any tethered raptor possessed under this permit must be maintained in accordance with the Federal falconry standards for "facilities and equipment" described in §21.29(g) unless a specific exception in writing is obtained. For untethered raptors, the breeding facilities must be soundly constructed and entirely enclosed with wood, wire netting, or other suitable material which provides a safe, healthy environment. The design of such facilities and ancillary equipment must—

    (i) Minimize the risk of injury by providing protection from predators, disturbances that would likely cause harm, extreme weather conditions, and collision with interior or perimeter construction materials and equipment such as support poles, windows, wire netting, perches, or lights;

    (ii) Enhance sanitation by providing a well-drained floor, fresh air ventilation, source of light, fresh water for bathing and drinking, access for cleaning, and interior construction materials suitable for thorough cleaning or disinfection; and

    (iii) Enhance the welfare and breeding success of the raptors by providing suitable perches, nesting and feeding sites, and observation ports or inspection windows during times when disturbance is felt to be undesirable.

(2) *Incubation of eggs.* Each permittee must notify the Director in writing within 5 days from the day the first egg is laid by any raptor held under a raptor propagation permit, but notice is not required more often than once every 60 days.

(3) *Marking requirements.* Every raptor possessed under this permit must be banded with a numbered, nonreusable marker provided by the Service or with a marker provided

by the competent wildlife management authority of a foreign country that meets the following Service marking standards:

   (i) Any raptor taken from the wild or hatched from an egg taken from the wild must be banded with a black, adjustable marker.

  (ii) Any captive-bred raptor must be banded by 2 weeks of age with either a yellow adjustable marker or a numbered seamless marker.

 (iii) Any permittee who wants to use a numbered seamless marker provided by the Service—

     (A) Must place the marker on the raptor's leg (*metatarsus*) before full growth is attained.

     (B) Must use as a marker with an opening (diameter) which is small enough to prevent its removal when the raptor is fully grown without causing serious injury to the raptor or damaging the marker's integrity or one-piece construction;

     (C) May band a raptor with more than one size marker when the potential diameter of the raptor's leg at maturity cannot be determined at the time of banding; and

     (D) Must remove all but one marker from any raptor with more than one marker before the raptor is 5 weeks of age and immediately return each marker that is removed to the Director.

  (iv) Each permittee must submit a report of marking to the Director within 5 days of such activity. The report must contain the date of marking; marker number(s); and the species, sex and age of the raptor.

(4) *Taking Raptors or Raptor Eggs from the Wild.* Any permit authorizing the permittee to take raptors or raptor eggs from the wild for propagation purposes is subject to the following additional restrictions:

   (i) The State in which the raptors or raptor eggs are taken must authorize the permittee in writing to take raptors or raptor eggs from the wild for propagation purposes; and

  (ii) No raptor listed in §17.11 of this chapter as "endangered" or "threatened" may be taken from the wild without first obtaining the proper permit under Part 17 of this chapter.

(5) *Transfer, purchase, sale, or barter of raptors, raptor eggs, or raptor semen.*

  (i) A permittee may transfer any lawfully possessed raptor, raptor egg, or raptor semen to another permittee or transfer any raptor to a falconer who holds a valid State falconry permit if no money or other consideration is involved.

  (ii) A permittee may transfer, purchase, sell, or barter any raptor which is banded with a numbered seamless marker provided or authorized by the Service, subject to the following conditions:

    (A) When the permittee purchases from, sells to, or barters with any person in the U.S., that person must be authorized under this part to purchase, sell, or barter captive-bred raptors;

    (B) When the permittee purchases from or barters with any person in a foreign country, that person must be authorized by the competent wildlife management authority of the foreign country in which the transaction occurs to sell or barter captive-bred raptors; and

    (C) When the permittee transfers to, sells to, or barters with any person in a foreign country, that person must be authorized to possess, purchase, or barter captive-bred raptors by the competent wildlife management authority of his/her country of residence or domicile and the same wildlife management authority must certify in writing that the recipient is an experienced falconer or raptor propagator who is required to maintain any raptors in his/her possession under conditions that are comparable to the conditions under which a permittee must maintain raptors under §21.29 or §21.30. No certification is required if the competent wildlife management authority itself is the recipient of captive-bred raptors for conservation purposes.

  (iii) No raptor may be traded, transferred, purchased, sold, or bartered until it is two weeks old and only after it is properly banded with a nonreusable marker provided or authorized by the Service, unless it is transferred, sold, or bartered to a State or Federal

wildlife management agency for conservation purposes.

(iv) A permittee may purchase, sell, or barter semen collected from any captive-bred raptor.

(v) A permittee may not purchase, sell, or barter any
raptor eggs, any raptors taken from the wild, any
raptor semen collected from the wild, or any raptors
hatched from eggs taken from the wild.

(6) *Use in falconry.* Permittees may use a raptor possessed for
propagation in the sport of falconry only if such use is
designated in both the propagation permit and the permittee's State falconry permit.

(7) *Interspecific hybridization.* Hybridization between species (interspecific hybridization) is authorized only if each
raptor produced by interspecific hybridization is either
imprinted on humans (hand-raised in isolation from the
sight of other raptors from 2 weeks of age until it is fully
feathered) or surgically sterilized.

(8) *Possession of dead raptors, non-viable eggs, nests, and
feathers.*

(i) Upon the death of any raptor held under permit, a
permittee must remove the marker and immediately
return it to the Director. The carcass must be de-
stroyed immediately, unless the permittee requests
authorization from the Director to retain possession
of it. A permittee who has obtained written authorization from the Director to retain possession of the
carcass may transfer it to any other person authorized
by the Service to possess it, provided no money or
other consideration is involved.

(ii) A permittee may possess addled or blown eggs, nests,
and feathers from raptors held under permit and may
transfer any of these items to any other person authorized by the Service to possess them provided no money
or other consideration is involved.

(9) *Intentional release to the wild.*

(i) A permittee must obtain written authorization from
the Director before intentionally releasing any raptor
to the wild. The raptor marker must be removed from
each bird and immediately returned to the Director.
A Federal bird band must be attached to each raptor
by a person designated by the Director before its
release.

(ii) No raptor produced by interspecific hybridization may be intentionally released to the wild.

(10) *Recordkeeping.* A permittee must maintain complete and accurate records of all operations, to include the following:

  (i) Acquisition of raptors, eggs, or semen from sources other than production.

    (A) Description of stock:

      1. Species, sex, age of each (if applicable).

      2. Genotype-natal area (geographical breeding site or area that captive stock represents, e.g., Colville River, Alaska; unknown; migrant taken in Maryland, etc.) and

      3. Marker number (if applicable).

    (B) Type of stock (including number or amount):

      1. Semen,

      2. Egg, or

      3. Bird.

    (C) How acquired:

      1. Purchase, barter, or transfer (include the purchase price or a description of any other consideration involved), or

      2. Taken from the wild.

    (D) Date acquired: month, day, and year.

    (E) From whom or where stock acquired:

      1. Name, address, and permit number of seller, barterer, or transferor; or

      2. Location where stock taken from the wild.

  (ii) Disposition of raptors, eggs, or semen.

    (A) Description of stock:

      1. Species, sex, age of each (if applicable),

      2. Geotype-natal area (geographical breeding site or area that captive stock represents, e.g., Colville River, Alaska; unknown; migrant taken in Maryland, etc.), and

      3. Marker number (if applicable).

    (B) Type of stock (including number or amount):

      1. Semen,

      2. Egg, or

      3. Bird.

    (C) Manner of disposition:

      1. Sale, barter, or transfer (include the sale price or a description of any other consideration involved),

2. Live loss,
3. Intentional release to the wild, or
4. Death.

(D) Date of disposition: month, day, and year.

(E) To whom or where stock disposed:
1. Name, address, and permit number of purchaser, barterer, or transferree, or
2. Description and location of other disposition.

(iii) Production and pedigree record.

(A) Mother and father(s):
1. Species,
2. Genotype-natal area, and
3. Marker number.

(B) Insemination:
1. Natural,
2. Artificial, or
3. Combined.

(C) Eggs laid:
1. Total,
2. First date, and
3. Last date.

(D) Eggs hatched:
1. Total,
2. First date, and
3. Last date.

(E) Young raised to 2 weeks of age:
1. Total produced, and
2. Marker number and date marked for each raptor.

(11) *Annual Report.* A permittee must submit an annual report by January 31 of each year for the preceding year to the Director. The report must include the following information for each species possessed by the permittee:

(i) Number of raptors possessed as of December 31.
(ii) Number of females laying eggs.
(iii) Number of eggs laid.
(iv) Number of eggs hatched.
(v) Number of young raised to 2 weeks of age.
(vi) Number of raptors sold or bartered by species.

(e) *Tenure of permit.* The tenure of raptor propagation permits is 5 years from the date of issuance, unless a shorter period of time is prescribed in the permit.

[48 FR 31608, July 8, 1983]

17

Fact Sheet Federal/State Qualifying Examination for a Falconry Permit

U.S. Department of the Interior
Fish and Wildlife Service

Purpose

The examination is designed to determine the applicant's knowledge of raptor identification, natural history, care in captivity, falconry techniques, and applicable laws and regulations.

Legal Requirement

Persons desiring to obtain a Federal/State falconry permit are required to answer correctly at least 80 percent of the questions on a supervised examination. A higher passing score may be established by the State wildlife agency. States may use either an examination provided by the Fish and Wildlife Service or a State examination approved by the Service.

Once an applicant has passed the examination, no future examination is required by Federal regulation for permit renewal or for changes in permit class or State of residence. State wildlife agencies may require additional examinations.

Administering Agency

State wildlife agency personnel or their representatives will administer the examination.

Content — F W 3 Series 0.'0 Examination

The examination consists of 100 multiple-choice questions, each with four possible answers. The questions are distributed into three general categories: raptor identification/biology — 25 percent; maintenance of raptors in captivity — 50 percent; and falconry practices/regulations — 25 percent.

A more detailed distribution of questions on this examination is provided by subject. Many of the questions fall into more than one category; e.g., a definition of "eyass" would need to be known to answer a question concerning the handling of eyasses.

	No. of
Subject	*Questions*
Literature Review/Definitions	4
Raptor Biology	
Species/Sex/Age Identification	4
Ecology (Habitat/Food/Behavior/Distribution)	10
Breeding Biology	5
Falconry	
Equipment and Facilities	12
Taking and Initial Handling of Raptors	8
General Health Factors/Food/Water	20
Injuries/Disease Parasites	15
Training/Hunting Practices	12
Ethics	4
Regulations	5
Other	1

Persons intending to take the examination should review the raptor literature and applicable regulations. The questions emphasize the practical aspects and obligations of being a falconer. A knowledge of scientific names and obscure publications is not required. The statistical probability of scoring 80 percent or more by chance alone is less than one in a million. If an applicant must guess the correct answer to 50 of the 100 questions, the probability of achieving a passing score is less than 5 in 1,000.

Failure to Pass

A person who fails the examination may apply to retake this or a similar examination. The schedule for reexamination will be determined by the State wildlife agency.

18

Whither Falconry?

FORTUNATELY, FEDERAL LAWS and most state laws now ban the killing of almost all birds of prey. It has been finally realized that they represent part of the chain that holds together the balance of nature, and the little damage they do to domestic fowl and game birds is far outweighed by their service in the control of rodents and other birds.

Rules for falconers set up by the federal government and many of the states are mainly sensible, requiring study, training, and licensing before the sport may be practiced. Unfortunately, the laws are still a mess of conflicting regulations where the capture, purchasing, and shipment of falcons and other hunting hawks are concerned.

A newcomer today who seriously wants to become a falconer usually can do so if he or she reads enough about the sport and proves to the proper officials an adequate sense of responsibility and professionalism. Since there has to be an age requirement, the government and most states have at least chosen a sensible one, ranging from fourteen to sixteen. If this were not required, every kid with an urge to walk around with a hawk on his or her shoulder would be carrying a sparrow hawk or a red-tailed hawk, neither of which makes a very good hunter. There is a lot to be learned about the proper care and feeding of a raptor. If everyone were allowed to take any young hawk from a nest or to trap any migrating hawk, a good many would die from mistreatment and malnutrition. We have come a long way from when I was a youngster in New York and in New Mexico where almost any kid could find a hawk nest. I raised not only Cooper's hawks and sharp-shinned hawks for hunting, but also red-tails, red-shouldered, and broad-winged hawks by the dozens. They were not hunters but made interesting pets, as did the tiny and beautifully colored sparrow hawks. We displayed them in the hawk and owl exhibits at Trailside Museum at Bear Mountain, New York. I also raised ospreys, just to see what they were like. I found them not especially bright. They refused to be carried about and were worth nothing as a hunting bird. The marsh hawk, too, was a fair pet. I found it unsuited to hunting. Its smaller feet and habit of flying close to the ground made it an interesting bird to fly, but it was really most concerned with field mice.

My greatest successes were with the big goshawks and the peregrine falcons. They are still — along with the prairie falcon and the gyrfalcon — the best hunting hawks available in North America today. (Peregrines from Mexico and prairie falcons can be purchased from a number of individuals, but the cost is very high. Falcons can be bought from overseas sources, but the cost is almost prohibitive. Only the wealthy falconer can afford a gyrfalcon today.)

Prairie falcon nests are more common in the West, but even there — mostly because of growing human population — they are becoming harder to locate.

At this time, the best bet for the amateur falconer is the small sharp-shinned hawk, the Cooper's hawk, and the goshawk, all native North American birds whose nests are found over most of the United States.

The brightest star on the horizon for American falconers is the current experimentation with breeding of captive falcons. This is being done, for example, at Cornell University under the supervision of Professor Tom Cade, by Dr. Heinz Meng of the State University of New York at New Paltz, and others. It was thought that birds of prey were far too wild to be bred in captivity. The hatching of Dr. Heinz Meng's one peregrine chick in May 1971 and the 20 young peregrines hatched and raised at Cornell University in 1973 changed all that.

Thanks to the Cornell program, the university established a "Peregrine Fund," which was allocated more than $100,000 for construction of a research facility. The developments came just in time for the peregrine. By 1970 it was estimated there were not more than 60 or 70 nesting sites in Mexico, all of the contiguous United States, and southern Canada. There were still a few hundred pairs, however, in Alaska and northwestern Canada.

Captive breeding has not been restricted just to the peregrine. Some success was reported with golden eagles and lanner falcons, an Old World version of the American prairie falcon. More experiments proved that red-shouldered hawks and the tiny American kestrel or sparrow hawk could be bred in captivity.

Years ago there were many peregrine nests in the center of New York City. (The chemical pesticides got to them because the songbirds they fed upon were filled with the poisons.) Releasing man-raised peregrines in such a metropolis might be an interesting experiment, particularly since most of their food would consist of city pigeons, which have never been subjected to much DDT and are relatively easy to catch.

Heinz Meng, a true pioneer in the captive breeding of peregrines and an ardent falconer himself, is eastern regional director of the North American Falconers Association. Meng first became interested in falcons in 1941, when he captured a peregrine he saw grab an immature marsh hawk on a beach. Thirty years later, he bred the first peregrines in captivity.

After his one bird was produced, he got seven in 1972 and seven more in 1973. He did it by removing eggs from a nest after a few days, putting them in an incubator, and destroying the nest. After a while, the falcons will nest again, so twice the number of chicks can be produced in one year.

"Falconry involves three hundred and sixty-five days a year," he says, "before anyone becomes a falconer. The passenger pigeon is extinct, because they were killed in great numbers for market, and nobody cared until after it was too late. The peregrine falcon is endangered, but falconers care — and they are *doing* something about the problem.

"Study of the birds of prey leads to understanding. People who might now go out and shoot a hawk because they have been taught it's bad would have a different attitude if they had any close association with one of the birds. If someone they knew kept a falcon or hawk, they'd say 'Oh, Joe's got one of those. It's a pretty good bird,' and they'd leave the wild birds alone.

"Pennsylvania has a good law. New York's new law is basically modelled after that law, but it will be better. In the New York law, a model regulation, a person has to pass rigid tests; then he must have all the facilities — hawk house, jesses, and hoods. The facilities must be inspected by a practiced falconer before a license to keep the birds will be granted.

"A lot of people ask, 'Where do you get a bird of prey?' Well, if you know all about the birds, you'll know where to get one. People will have to know these things — where to get the birds and how to get food for them — before they are permitted to be falconers.

"A lot of people think goshawks are enemies of game birds, but the fact is that they actually increase game-bird populations. They may eat a grouse now and then, but they eat a lot more crows, squirrels, skunks and raccoons — all of which eat grouse eggs. So the end result is that by keeping other predators down, goshawks actually help birds."

Objections to falconry as a "cruel" sport can be dismissed as childish. A falcon or an accipiter hawk, when it kills for food, is doing what it does naturally. The falconer is not the hunter. All the falconer does is teach the hawk to be tolerant of the presence of man. The hunting falcon is doing nothing more than it would be doing if it were wild. Since the falconer feeds it most of the year, it takes less of a toll of wild birds and small game than if it were wild itself. If falconry is cruel — or if the falcon itself is cruel — then nature is cruel. But then nature is the way it is and no amount of emotionalism can change that.

There is a great awakening of interest in falconry in North America today, and it is possible the sport may attain some of its former greatness. Birds raised in captivity are now available to falconers. If one is lost while hunting, it might at least be considered a restocked bird and may well find a mate and reproduce naturally.

There is still a considerable amount of stuffiness on the part of the larger falconry associations, probably because falconry has long been considered an "exclusive" sport. But even the publicity-shy officials of these organizations cannot stop the resurgence of interest in the sport. Ardent beginners will get their training and their hawks.

19

Bibliography

G. Ronald Austing, *The World Of The Red-Tailed Hawk*. J.B. Lippincott Co., Philadelphia, 1964.

Frank Lyman Beebe and Harold Melvin Webster, *North American Falconry and Hunting Hawks*. World Press, Inc., Denver, Colo. 1964–1972.

Frank Lyman Beebe, *Hawks, Falcons and Falconry*. Hancock House, Seattle, Wash. and New York, 1976.

Arthur Cleveland Bent, *Life Histories of North American Birds of Prey*. (In two parts.) Dover Publications, New York. (Reprinted, 1961.)

Gilbert Blaine, *Falconry*. (Sportsman's Library, Vol. XV.) Philip Alan, London, 1936.

Leslie Brown and Dean Amadon, *Eagles, Hawks & Falcons of The World*. McGraw-Hill, New York, 1968.

Dr. Tom J. Cade, *Ecology of the Peregrine and Gyrfalcon Populations in Alaska*. University of California Press, Berkeley, 1960.

Humphrey ap Evans, *Falconry*. Arco Publishing Co., New York, 1974.

Louis Agassiz Fuertes, "Falconry, the Sport of Kings." *National Geographic*, December 1920. (This issue can be found in your local library.)

Frederick II of Hohenstaufen, *The Art of Falconry*. (De Arte Venandi Cum

Avibus.) Translated by Dr. Casey A. Wood and F. Marjorie Fyfe, Stanford University Press, Stanford, Calif., 1943.

Phillip Glasier, *As the Falcon Her Bells.* Heinemann, London, 1963.

James Edmund Harting, *Hints On The Management of Hawks.* Thames Valley Press, Maidenhead, England, 1971.

Dr. E. W. Jameson, Jr., *The Hawking of Japan.* (Privately printed at Davis, California, 1962.)

John Kaufmann and Heinz Meng, *Falcon's Return.* William Morrow & Co., New York, 1975.

J.G. Mavrogordato, *A Hawk for the Bush.* H. F. and G. Witherby, Ltd., London, 1960.

E. B. Mitchell, *The Art and Practice of Hawking.* Charles T. Branford Co., Boston, Mass. (Reprinted, 1959.)

Lt. Col. E. Delmé Radcliffe, *Falconry — Notes On Falconidae Used In India In Falconry.* Seven Corners Press Ltd. Guilfors, Surrey, England, 1971.

William F. Russell, Jr. *Falconry, A Handbook for Hunters.* Charles Scribner's Sons, New York, 1940.

Francis Henry Salvin and William Brodrick, *Falconry in The British Isles.* Tabard Press Ltd., London, 1970.

Ronald Stevens, *Observations on Modern Falconry.* (Privately printed by author, 1956.)

Ronald Stevens, *The Taming of Genghis.* Faber and Faber, London, 1956.

M. H. Woodford, *A Manual of Falconry.* Adam and Charles Black, London, 1960.

20

State Information Officers

Alabama
Chief, Information and Education
Department of Conservation and
Natural Resources
64 North Union Street
Montgomery, AL 36104

Alaska
Education and Information Officer
Department of Fish and Game
P.O. Box 3-2000
Juneau, AK 99802

Arizona
Chief, Information and Education
Game and Fish Department
2222 West Greenway
Phoenix, AZ 85023

Arkansas
Chief, Information and Education
Game and Fish Commission
#2 Natural Resources Drive
Little Rock, AR 72205

California
Director
Fish and Game Commission
1416 Ninth Street
Sacramento, CA 95814

Colorado
Director
Division of Wildlife
6060 Broadway
Denver, CO 80216

Connecticut
Chief, Wildlife Unit
Department of Environmental
Protection
State Office Building
165 Capitol Avenue
Hartford, CT 06115

Delaware
Director
Division of Fish and Wildlife
89 Kings Highway
P.O. Box 1401
Dover, DE 19903

District of Columbia
Director
Department of Environmental
Services
5000 Overlook Ave. S.W.
Washington, DC 20032

Florida
Chief of Information — Education
Game and Fresh Water Fish
Commission
620 South Meridian Street
Tallahassee, FL 32301

Georgia
Director
Game and Fish Division
270 Washington Street, S.W.
Atlanta, GA 30334

Hawaii
Director
Division of Forestry and Wildlife
1151 Punchbowl Street
Honolulu, HI 96813

Idaho
Chief, Information and Education
Fish and Game Department

600 South Walnut
Box 25
Boise, ID 83707

Illinois
Supervisor, Information/Education
Services
Department of Conservation
Lincoln Tower Plaza,
524 S. Second St.
Springfield, IL 62706

Indiana
Head, Division of Fish and Wildlife
Department of Natural Resources
608 State Office Building
Indianapolis, IN 46204

Iowa
Chief of Fish and Game
Wallace State Office Building
300 4th Street
Des Moines, IA 50319

Kansas
Chief, Game Division
Fish and Game Commission
Box 54A, RR 2
Pratt, KS 67124

Kentucky
Director, Division of Game
Management
Department of Fish and Wildlife
Resources
#1 Game Farm Road
Frankfort, KY 40601

Louisiana
Information Officer
Department of Wildlife and
Fisheries
400 Royal Street
New Orleans, LA 70130

Maine
Director, Information and Education
Department of Inland Fisheries
and Wildlife
284 State St., Station #41
Augusta, ME 04333

Maryland
Chief, Public Information Service
Department of Natural Resources
Tawes State Office Building
Annapolis, MD 21401

Massachusetts
Director, Audio Visual Aids
Division of Fisheries and Wildlife
100 Cambridge Street
Boston, MA 02202

Michigan
Chief, Wildlife Division
Box 30028
Lansing, MI 48909

Minnesota
Director, Division of Fish and
Wildlife
Department of Natural Resources
300 Centennial Building
658 Cedar Street
St. Paul, MN 55155

Mississippi
Chief of Game
Department of Wildlife
Conservation
Southport Mall
Post Office Box 451
Jackson, MS 39205

Missouri
Chief, Wildlife Division
Department of Conservation
Post Office Box 180
Jefferson City, MO 65102

Montana
Administrator, Environment and
Information Division
Department of Fish, Wildlife and
Parks
1420 E. Sixth
Helena, MT 59601

Nebraska
Chief of Information and Education
Game and Parks Commission
2200 North 33rd Street
Post Office Box 30370
Lincoln, NE 68503

Nevada
Public Information Officer
Department of Wildlife
Box 10678
Reno, NV 89520

New Hampshire
Chief, Conservation, Education
and Information Division
Fish and Game Department
34 Bridge Street
Concord, NH 03301

New Jersey
Director
Division of Fish, Game and
Wildlife
Labor and Industry Building
CN 400
Trenton, NJ 08625

New Mexico
Information and Education Officer
Game and Fish Department
Villagra Building
Santa Fe, NM 87503

New York
Public Information Officer
Department of Environmental
Conservation
50 Wolf Road
Albany, NY 12233

North Carolina
Executive Director
Wildlife Resources Commission
Archdale Building
512 North Salisbury Street
Raleigh, NC 27611

North Dakota
Chief, Information – Education
Division
State Game and Fish Department
2121 Lovett Avenue
Bismarck, ND 58505

Ohio
Chief, Information Division
Department of Natural Resources
Fountain Square
Columbus, OH 43224

Oklahoma
Chief, Information – Education
Division
Department of Wildlife Conservation
1801 North Lincoln
Post Office Box 53465
Oklahoma City, OK 73152

Oregon
Chief, Information and Education
Department of Fish and Wildlife
Box 3503
Portland, OR 97208

Pennsylvania
Chief, Information
Game Commission
Post Office Box 1567
Harrisburg, PA 17120

Rhode Island
Information and Education Officer
Department of Environmental
Management
83 Park Street
Providence, RI 02903

South Carolina
Division of Information and
Public Affairs
Wildlife and Marine Resources
Department
1015 Main Street
Box 167
Columbia, SC 29202

South Dakota
Supervisor of Information and
Education
Department of Game, Fish and Parks
445 East Capitol
Pierre, SD 57501

Tennessee
Chief, Information and Education
Wildlife Resources Agency
Post Office Box 40747
Ellington Agricultural Center
Nashville, TN 37204

Texas
Director, Information/Education
Parks and Wildlife Department
4200 Smith School Road
Austin, TX 78744

Utah
Chief, Information and Education
Division of Wildlife Resources
1596 N.W. Temple
Salt Lake City, UT 84116

Vermont
Information and Education Specialist
Fish and Game Department
Montpelier, VT 05602

Virginia
Chief, Education Division
Commission of Game and Inland
Fisheries
4010 West Broad Street
Box 11104
Richmond, VA 23230

Washington
Director
Department of Game
600 North Capitol Way
Olympia, WA 98504

West Virginia
Chief of Information and Education
Department of Natural Resources
1800 Washington Street East
Charleston, WV 25305

Wisconsin
Director, Bureau of Information
and Education
Department of Natural Resources
Box 7921
Madison, WI 53707

Wyoming
Chief, Information and Education
Game and Fish Department
Cheyenne, WY 82002

21

Falconry Associations

North American Falconry
Association
11985 Onieda Road
Grand Ledge, MI 48837
(2,000 members)

Affiliated Clubs
British Columbia Falconry
Association
c/o D.W. Waynes, Secretary
18140 72nd Avenue
Surry BC V3S 4P1
Canada

Colorado Hawking Club
P.O. Box 370
Ft. Collins, CO 80522

Florida Hawking Fraternity
612 Timberwolf Trail
Apopka, FL 32703

Great Lakes Falconers Association
c/o Larry Miller, Secretary
P.O. Box 121
Warrenville, IL 60555

Idaho Falconer's Association
Rt. 3, Hialeah Drive
Eagle, ID 83616

Indiana Falconers Association
c/o James Mills
16655 Gerald Street
Granger, IN 46530

Jersey Falconry Club
c/o James Yoson
144 Maple St.
Bridgewater, NJ 08807

Kentucky Falconers Association
4811 Partridge Run
Louisville, KY 40213

Louisiana Hawking Club
c/o Thomas Coulson, President
2134 Mehle Avenue
Arabi, LA 70032

Massachusetts Falconry &
Hawk Trust
c/o Scott Keniston, L.O.
Rt. 2, Box 761
Winterport, MA 04496

Montana Falconers Association
c/o Jeff Waldum, Treasurer
Box 13
Browning, MT 59417

North Carolina Hawking Club
P.O. Box 12621
Research Triangle Park, NC 27709

Foreign Clubs
Association Nationale
Des Falconniers
Et Autoursiers
Gilles Nortier
3, Route de Saint-Nabor
67530 Ottrott
France

British Falconers' Club
Dr. N. Fox, Wildlife Department
Dyfed College of Art
Carmarthen, Dyfed
Wales, Great Britain

Club "Marie de Bourgogne"
Patrick Morel, Secretary
Rue Kievit 23
3070 Kortenberg
Belgium

Deutscher Falkenorden
c/o Herr H.J. Dreyer
Kieler Strasse 15
2056 Reinbek
West Germany

Osterr, Falknerbund
Postfach 221
1011 Vienna
Austria

Nederlandsh Falkeniers-
Verbund "Adriaan Mollen"
Heer W.P.J. Lammers, Secretary
Vincent V. Goghstraat 1
Lisse 1660
Holland

Schweizerische
Falkner-Vereinigung
F. Michel, Birkenweg 24
3800 Matten B. Interlaken
Switzerland

Welsh Hawking Club
Ann Shuttleworth, Editor
Austringer 21, N. Close
Blackfordby
North Burton-on-Trent
Staffordshire
England

Zimbabwe Falconer's Club
P.O. Box 8564
Causeway
Zimbabwe

Index